A POCKET GUIDE

WALES IN QUOTATION

A POCKET GUIDE

WALES IN QUOTATION

MEIC STEPHENS

UNIVERSITY OF WALES PRESS
THE WESTERN MAIL
1999

Published by the University of Wales Press and The Western Mail

ISBN 0-7083-1560-7

A catalogue record for this book is available from the British Library

Cover illustration by Jonathan Adams
Cover design by Chris Neale
Typeset at the University of Wales Press
Printed by Dinefwr Press, Llandybïe

Contents

Introduction

'Who speaks for Wales?' asked Raymond Williams in 1971. 'Nobody. That is both the problem and the encouragement.' There is in this country a tradition of dissent and argument, so that voices are often raised with passion and eloquence on matters affecting the life of the Welsh people. Many are to be heard in this selection of quotations about Wales and the Welsh from Roman times to our own day.

They have been drawn from a wide variety of sources, mostly Welsh, English and Latin. Some are complimentary, some critical, and a number are hostile to both people and country. The Welsh have often had a bad press in England, a fact we should not ignore when trying to understand our relationship with our closest neighbours, although we should not make too much of it; it is, after all, proof of our difference.

The quotations, more than a thousand in all, are arranged in chronological order, and the progress of Welsh history can be heard throughout. They refer, for the most part, to the characteristics of the Welsh – our language, our literature, our religion, our social customs, our political aspirations, and so on – and especially to our sense of national identity and nationhood. In particular, they trace the movement towards Welsh self-government which passed a significant milestone with the creation of our National Assembly in May 1999. From now on we Welsh can define ourselves on home ground.

The reader looking for a larger selection of quotations about Wales and the Welsh will find it in my book *A Most Peculiar People*, published by the University of Wales Press in 1992.

Meic Stephens   June 1999
Whitchurch
Cardiff

Notes for the Reader

Multiple quotations from the same source have the full source noted after the first entry only,

An asterisk indicates that the quotation has been translated from the original language (usually Welsh or Latin, but also French, German and Irish).

1   All the Britons paint themselves with woad, which gives their skin a bluish colour and makes them look very dreadful in battle.*

Julius Caesar, Commentarii de Bello Gallico, 51 BC

2   The Silures were not . . . easily quelled. Neither lenity nor rigorous measures could induce them to submit.*

Tacitus, Annales, c.115

3   The druids were ranged in order, with hands uplifted, invoking the gods and pouring forth horrible imprecations. The strangeness of the sight struck the Romans with awe and terror.*

4   Britain, abandoned by the Romans, passed into the power of the Saxons.*

Chronica Gallica, 440

5   The battle of Badon, in which Arthur carried the Cross of our Lord Jesus Christ for three days and three nights on his shoulders and the Britons were victors.*

Annales Cambriae, 516

6   Ever since it was first inhabited, Britain has been ungratefully rebelling, stiff-necked and haughty, now against God, now against its own countrymen.*

Gildas, De Excidio et Conquestu Britanniae, c.540

7   Britain has kings, but they are tyrants; she has judges, but they are wicked. Britain has priests, but they are fools; very many ministers, but they are shameless; clerics, but they are treacherous grabbers.*

8   The kinsmen of yonder strange-tongued man whose voice I heard across the river setting on his dogs will obtain possession of this place, and it will be theirs, and they will hold it for themselves.*

St Beuno, on hearing a Saxon on the bank of the Severn,
mid-sixth century, recorded in Llyfr Ancr Llanddewibrefi, 1346

9   Noble brothers and sisters, be glad, and guard your faith and religion, and do the little things which you have heard from me, and which I have shown you. And fare you well, and may your conduct be steadfast on earth. For we shall never meet here again.*

St David, c.589

10 The wide host of England sleep with light in their eyes,
    And those who had not fled were braver than were wise.*
                    Taliesin, 'Marwnad Owain ab Urien', late sixth cent.
                                            (trans. Anthony Conran)

11 Men went to Catraeth, keen was their company.
    They were fed on fresh mead, and it proved poison –
    Three hundred warriors ordered for warfare,
    And after the revelling there was silence.*
                    Aneirin, *Y Gododdin*, *c.* 600 (trans. Anthony Conran)

12 Although they were being slain, they slew;
    Till the world ends they will be honoured . . .
    They bore no disgrace, men who stood firm.*

13 The poets of the people will judge who are the men of
                                                    courage.*

14 Aethelfrith led his army to Chester and there slew numberless
Welshmen, and so was fulfilled the prophecy of Augustine,
wherein he said, If the Welsh will not be at peace with us, they
shall perish at the hand of the Saxons.
                            The Anglo-Saxon Chronicle, *c.*615

15 There are in Britain, corresponding with the five books of the
divine law, five languages and four nations – English, British,
Scots and Picts. Each of these has its own language, but all are
united in the study of God's truth by the fifth, Latin.*
                    Bede, *Historia Ecclesiastica Gentis Anglorum*, 731

16 The Britons for the most part have a natural hatred for the
English and uphold their own bad customs against the true Easter
of the Catholic Church; nevertheless, they are opposed by the
power of God and man alike.*

17 It is to this day the fashion among the Britons to reckon the
faith and religion of Englishmen as naught and to hold no more
converse with them than with the heathen.*

18 The scholars of the island of Britain had no skill and set down
no record in writing. I have therefore made a heap of all that I
have found.*

                                    Historia Brittonum, *c.*830

2

19   The Welsh will rise: they will give battle.*

Anonymous, 'Armes Prydein', c.930 (trans. Joseph P. Clancy)

20   The Welsh must become, through warfare,
Trained troops, united, one band, sworn brothers.*

21   Let him who would be a leader be a bridge.*

*Pedair Cainc y Mabinogi, c.*1060

22   Gruffudd ap Llywelyn, golden-torqued king of the Welsh and their defender, died after many plunderings and victories against his foes, after many feasts and delights, and great gifts of gold and silver and costly raiment, he who was sword and shield over the fate of all Wales.*

entry for 1063, *Brenhinedd y Saeson*

23   The Welsh are entirely different in nation, language, laws and habits, judgements and customs.*

The Bishop of St David's, in letter to Pope Innocent II, c.1137

24   This nation, O King, may now, as in former times, be harassed, and in a great measure weakened and destroyed by your and other powers, and it will also prevail by its laudable exertions, but it can never be totally subdued through the wrath of man, unless the wrath of God shall concur. Nor do I think that any other nation than this of Wales, or any other language, whatever may hereafter come to pass, shall on the day of severe examination before the Supreme Judge, answer for this corner of the earth.*

Old man of Pencader to Henry II in 1163, recorded by Giraldus Cambrensis, *Descriptio Kambriae*, 1193

25   A people called Welsh, so bold and ferocious that, when unarmed, they do not fear to encounter an armed force, being ready to shed their blood in defence of their country, and to sacrifice their lives for renown.*

Henry II in letter to the Emperor of Byzantium, c.1165

26   At Christmas in that year the Lord Rhys ap Gruffudd held court in splendour at Cardigan, in the castle. And he set two kinds of contests there: one between bards and poets, another between harpists and crowders and pipers and various classes of music-craft. And he had two chairs set for the victors.*

entry for 1176, *Brut y Tywysogion*

27   My fellow countrymen, the Welsh, although wholly treacherous to everyone – to each other as well as to foreigners – covet freedom, neglect peace, are warlike and skilful in arms, and eager for revenge.*

Walter Map, *De Nugis Curialium*, *c*.1180

28   The Welsh are all, by nature,
Wilder than the beasts of the field.*

Chrétien de Troyes, *Le Roman de Perceval*, 1181–90

29   As Dyfed with its seven cantrefi is the fairest of all the lands of Wales, as Pembrokeshire is the fairest part of Dyfed, and this spot the fairest of Pembroke, it follows that Manorbier is the sweetest spot in Wales.*

Giraldus Cambrensis (a native of Manorbier),
Itinerarium Kambriae, 1191

30   The perpetual remembrance of their former greatness, the recollection of their Trojan descent, and the high and continued majesty of the kingdom of Britain, may draw forth many a latent spark of animosity and encourage the daring spirit of rebellion.*

31   The Welsh esteem noble birth and generous descent above all things . . . Even the common people know their family trees by heart and can readily recite the list of their ancestors . . . back to the sixth or seventh generation.*

32   They are as easy to overcome in a single battle as they are difficult to subdue in a protracted war.*

33   If they could be inseparable, they would be insuperable.*

34   The English fight for power, the Welsh for liberty; the one to procure gain, the other to avoid loss; the English hirelings for money, the Welsh patriots for their country.*

35   Nature has given not only to the highest, but also to the inferior classes of this nation a boldness and a confidence in speaking and answering, even in the presence of their princes and chieftains.*

36   It is to be observed that the British language is more subtle and richer in north Wales, that country being less intermixed with

foreigners. Many, however, assert that the language of Ceredigion in south Wales is the most refined.*

37   In their rhymed songs and set speeches they are so subtle and ingenious that they produce, in their native tongue, ornaments of wonderful and exquisite invention both in the words and the syntax.*

38   In their musical concerts they do not sing in unison like the inhabitants of other countries, but in many different parts . . . You will hear as many different parts and voices as there are performers who all at length unite with organic melody.*

39   They do not engage in marriage until they have tried, by previous cohabitation, the disposition, and particularly the fecundity, of the person with whom they are engaged.*

40   No one of this nation ever begs, for the houses of all are common to all, and they consider liberality and hospitality among the first virtues.*

41   Happy and fortunate indeed would be this nation, nay completely blessed, if it had good prelates and pastors, and but one prince, and that prince a good one.*

42   I am sprung from the princes of Wales and from the barons of the Marches, and when I see injustice in either race, I hate it.*
Giraldus Cambrensis, *De Invectibus,* 1216

43   It is not easy in our part of Wales to control Welshmen except by one of their own kind.*
his vassals to the Earl of Pembroke, 1244

44   The gentlefolk of Wales, despoiled of their liberty and rights, came to Llywelyn ap Gruffudd and revealed to him, with tears, their grievous bondage to the English, and made known to him that they preferred to be slain in battle for their liberty than to suffer themselves to be unrighteously trampled upon by foreigners.*
entry for 1256, *Brut y Tywysogion*

45   Wales at this time was in a most straitened condition, and owing to the cessation of agriculture, commerce and the tending of flocks, the inhabitants began to waste away through want;

unwillingly, too, did they bend to the yoke of the English laws; their ancient pride of nobility faded and even the harp of the ecclesiastics was turned to grief and lamentation.*

Matthew Paris, *Chronica Majora*, 1256

46   Far from showing obedience to the king's son, Edward, [the Welsh] only ridiculed and heaped insults upon him, and he in consequence conceived the idea of giving up Wales and the Welsh as untameable.*

47   The King well knows that the rights of Llywelyn's principality are entirely separate from those of the King's realm, although Llywelyn holds his principality under the King's royal power.*

Llywelyn ap Gruffudd in letter to Edward I, 11 July 1273

48   And then was effected the betrayal of Llywelyn in the belfry at Bangor by his own men.*

entry for 1282, *Brut y Tywysogion*

49   The King's host came without warning upon Llywelyn ap Gruffudd and slew him and many of his host on the feast day of Pope Damaseus, the eleventh day of the month of December, a Friday, and then all Wales was cast to the ground.*

entry for 1282, *Brenhinedd y Saeson*

50   Glory to God in the highest, peace to men of goodwill, mastery to the English, victory to Edward, honour to the Church, joy for the Christian faith and eternal oblivion for the Welsh. The good news has reached our ears that the old serpent Llywelyn, sometime prince of Wales, the father of all deceit, the child of revolt, the author of treason and chief of all evil, has been defeated on the field of battle.*

clerk to Edward I, December 1282

51   Know, sire, that Llywelyn ap Gruffudd is dead, his army broken and all the flower of his men killed.*

Roger Lestrange, in letter to Edward I, December 1282

52   The Divine Providence . . . has now wholly and entirely transferred under our proper dominion the land of Wales with its inhabitants . . . and has annexed and united the same into the Crown.*

the Statute of Rhuddlan, 1284

53   Welshmen are Welshmen.*

clerk at Beaumaris, February 1296

54   In this year King Edward of England made Lord Edward, his son and heir, Prince of Wales and Count of Chester. When the Welsh heard this, they were overjoyed, thinking him their lawful master, for he was born in their lands.*

entry for 1300, *Historia Anglicana*

55   When elsewhere it is summer, it is winter in Wales.*

Pierre de Langtoft, 1311

56   I will give myself up for the people, for it is better that one man should die than the whole people go into exile or perish by the sword.*

Llywelyn Bren, at his execution for having led a rising by the men of Glamorgan, 1317, quoted in *Fiesta Edwardi de Carnarvon*

57   A slender, exquisite lady of beautiful Welsh speech.*
Casnodyn, in poem to Gwenllian, wife of Sir Gruffudd Llwyd, *c*.1320

58   The Welsh habit of revolt against the English is a long-standing madness . . . and this is the reason. The Welsh, formerly called the Britons, were once noble, crowned with the whole realm of England; but they were expelled by the Saxons and lost both name and kingdom . . . But from the sayings of the prophet Merlin they still hope to recover England. Hence it is they frequently rebel.*

*Vita Edwardi Secundi, c.*1330

59   Englishmen were encouraged to intermingle with the Welsh so that the peace would be better assured and security improved by Englishmen so placed.

Calendar of Close Rolls, 1339–41

60   Since coming into Wales he has found the country most marvellous and strange.

John de Weston, to officers of the Prince of Wales, 21 August 1345

61   What care we for the barefoot rascals?
English parliamentarians' retort to Siôn Trefor, Bishop of St Asaph, when he put the case of Owain Glyndŵr against Reginald Grey, Lord of Ruthin, 1400

62 It is ordained . . . that no Englishman shall be convicted by any Welshman within the land of Wales. It is ordained . . . that from henceforth no Welshman shall be armed nor bear defensible armour. It is ordained that no Englishman married to a Welshman . . . shall be put into any office in Wales or in the Marches.*

Rotuli Parliamentorum, 1401

63 At Machynlleth, Owain [Glyndŵr] and his mountain men, even in their miserable plight, usurping the methods of conquerors and the rights of kings, although to his own confusion, held or simulated or pretended to hold parliaments.*

Adam of Usk, *Chronicon*, 1404

64 My nation has been trodden underfoot by the fury of the barbarous Saxons.*

Owain Glyndŵr, in letter to King Charles VI of France,
March 1406

65 Owain [Glyndŵr] went into hiding on St Matthew's Day in Harvest, and thereafter his hiding-place was unknown. Very many say that he died; the seers say that he did not.*

Annals of Owain Glyndŵr, 1415

66 Beware of Wales, Christ Jesus must us keep,
That it make not our child's child to weep.

The Libel of English Policy, *c*.1436

67 The red dragon will show the way.*

Deio ab Ieuan Du, in poem thanking Siôn ap Rhys
of Glyn Nedd for the gift of a bull, *c*.1450

68 Take Glamorgan and Gwynedd,
Make one land from Conwy to Neath,
If England's dukes resent it,
All Wales will rally to your side.*

Guto'r Glyn, to William Herbert, Earl of Pembroke, *c*.1450

69 Woe that we are born in servitude.*

in poem to Edward IV

70 The Welsh may now be said to have recovered their independence, for the most wise and fortunate Henry VII is a Welshman.*

Venetian envoy after the battle of Bosworth, 1485

71   I dwell with my people.*

Richard ap Hywel, on declining the offer of
rank and lands in England, 1485

72   His Highness [Henry VIII] . . . of the singular love and favour
that he bears towards his subjects of this said dominion of Wales,
and intending to reduce them to the perfect order, notice and
knowledge of the laws of this his realm, and utterly to extirpate all
and singular the sinister usages and customs differing from the
same . . . hath ordained, enacted and established that his said
country or dominion of Wales shall stand and continue for ever
from henceforth incorporated, united and annexed to and with his
Realm of England.

Act of Union, 1536

73   Persons born or to be born in the said Principality . . . of
Wales shall have and enjoy and inherit all and singular Freedoms,
Liberties, Rights, Privileges and Laws . . . as other the King's
subjects have, enjoy or inherit.

74   The people of the dominion [of Wales] have and do daily
use a speech nothing like nor consonant to the natural mother
tongue used within this realm . . . No person or persons that use
the Welsh speech or language shall have or enjoy any manor,
office or fees within the realm of England, Wales or other the
king's dominions upon pain of forfeiting the same offices or fees
unless he or they use and exercise the speech or language of
English.

75   Go barefoot on pilgrimage to his Grace the King and his
Council to beseech that the Holy Scriptures should be available in
your language. If you do not wish to be worse than animals . . .
obtain learning in your own language; if you do not wish to be
more unnatural than any other nation under the sun, love your
language and those who love it.*

William Salesbury, *Oll Synnwyr Pen Kembero Ygyd*, 1547

76   My distinguished lord, the heart of every Welshman leaps
with true joy when he hears a man of your eminence speaking his
language.*

Gruffydd Robert to the Earl of Pembroke, in
Dosparth byrr ar y rhan gyntaf o ramadeg gymraeg, 1567

77   You will have some people, as soon as they see the Severn or

the belfries of Shrewsbury, and hear an Englishman say good-morrow, who begin to abandon their Welsh.*

78   He who denies his father or his mother or his country or his language will never be a man of civilization and virtue.*

79   Take ten, he said, and call them Rice,
      Take another ten and call them Price,
      Take fifty others and call them Hughes,
      A hundred more and dub them Pughes,
      Now Roberts name a hundred score
      And Williams name a legion more,
      And call, he moaned in languid tones,
      Call all the others Jones.
                              Anonymous, attributed to a Tudor judge, *c.*1570,
                              quoted in H. Morris Jones, *Doctor in the Whip's Room*, 1955

80   Of late [the Welsh] are applying themselves to settle in towns, learn mechanics, engage in commerce, cultivate the soil, and undertake all other public duties equally with Englishmen.*
                              Humphrey Llwyd, *Commentarioli Descriptionis*
                              Britannicae Fragmentum, 1572

81   A better people to govern than the Welsh [Europe] holdeth not.
                              Sir Henry Sidney, in letter to Sir Francis Walsingham,
                              1 March 1583

82   Ye British poets, repeat in royal song
      (With weighty words used in King Arthur's days)
      Th'imperial stock from whence your Queen hath sprung;
      Install in verse your Princess' lasting praise:
          Pencerddiaid, play on ancient harp and crowde;
          Atceiniaid, sing her praises piercing loud.
                              Morris Kyffin, *The Blessedness of Britain*, 1587

83   Let hills and rocks rebounding echoes yield
      Of Queen Elizabeth's long lasting fame;
      Let woody groves and watery streams be filled,
      And creeks and caves, with sounding of the same:
          O Cambria, stretch and strain thy utmost breath
          To praise and pray for Queen Elizabeth.

84   The translation of the Bible into the Welsh or British tongue

which by Act of Parliament should long since have been done, is now performed by one Dr [William] Morgan and set forth in print.

Acts of the Privy Council, 22 September 1588

85   There is no doubt that likeness in religion is a far stronger bond of union than uniformity of language.

William Morgan, in preface to *Y Bibl Cyssegr-lan*, 1588

86   We have been long afflicted and oppressed
By those that sought our whole race to destroy.

John Davies of Hereford, 'Cambria', c. 1590

87   I speak for those who tongues are strange to thee
In thine own tongue: if my words be unfit,
That blame be mine; but if Wales better be
By my disgrace, I hold that grace to me.

88   I am a poor young man born and bred in the mountains of Wales.

John Penry in letter to Lord Burghley
shortly before his execution, 22 May 1593

89   A Churchman from Wales declared at the Eisteddfod that the printing of Welsh books should not be allowed, for the Welsh should be made to learn English, and to forget their Welsh . . . Could the Devil himself have expressed it better?*

Morris Kyffin, *Deffynniad Ffydd Eglwys Loegr*, 1594

90   A wretched people [the Welsh], they know little, have seen less, and they cannot be taught.*

91   In Wales, the true remnant of the ancient Britons, there are good authorities to show the long time they had poets, which they called bards: so through all the conquests of Romans, Saxons, Danes, and Normans, some of whom did seek to ruin all memory of learning among them, yet do their poets to this day, last; so as it is not more notable in soon beginning than in long continuing.

Sir Philip Sidney, *An Apology for Poetry*, 1595

92   But I will never be a truant, love,
Till I have learned thy language, for thy tongue
Makes Welsh as sweet as ditties highly penn'd

Sung by a fair queen in a summer's bower,
With ravishing division, to her lute.

Mortimer to Lady Mortimer,
William Shakespeare, Henry IV, part I, c.1597

93   Now I perceive the devil understands Welsh.

Hotspur

94   Lie still, ye thief, and hear the lady sing in Welsh.

Lady Percy to Hotspur

I had rather hear Lady my brach howl in Irish.

Hotspur to Lady Percy

95   Heaven defend me from that Welsh fairy! lest he transform me to a piece of cheese.

Falstaff of Sir Hugh Evans,
William Shakespeare, The Merry Wives of Windsor, 1597

96   I am not able to answer the Welsh flannel.

Falstaff

97   Though it appear a little out of fashion,
There is much care and valour in this Welshman.

King Henry of Fluellen,
William Shakespeare, Henry V, 1599

98   If your majesty is remembered of it, the Welshmen did good service in a garden where leeks did grow, wearing leeks in their Monmouth caps, which, your majesty knows, to this hour is an honourable badge of service; and, I do believe, your majesty takes no scorn to wear the leek upon St Tavy's day.

Fluellen to King Henry

I wear it for a memorable honour, for I am Welsh, good countryman.

King Henry to Fluellen

99   You thought, because he [Fluellen] could not speak English in the native garb he could not therefore handle an English cudgel: you find it otherwise; and henceforth let a Welsh correction teach you a good English condition.

Gower to Pistol

100   These mountains may not unfitly be termed the British Alps, as being the most vast of all Britain.

Anonymous, of Snowdonia, Description of Wales, 1599

101   No country in England so flourished in one hundred years as Wales has done since the government of Henry VII to this time, insomuch that if our fathers were now living they would think it some strange country inhabited with a foreign nation, so altered is the countryman, the people changed in heart within and the land altered in hue without, from evil to good, and from bad to better.

George Owen, *The Description of Pembrokeshire*, 1603

102   Remember the country has always been fruitful of loyal hearts to your majesty, a very garden and seed-plot of honest minds and men . . . Though the nation be said to be unconquered and most loving liberty, yet it was never mutinous, and please your majesty, but stout, valiant, courteous, hospitable, temperate, ingenious, capable of all good arts, most lovingly constant, charitable, great antiquaries, religious preservers of their gentry and genealogy, as they are zealous and knowing in religion.

Ben Jonson, *For the Honour of Wales*, 1619

103   It was Owain Glyndŵr's policy to bring all things to waste, that the English should find not the strength nor resting place in the country.

Sir John Wynn, *History of the Gwydir Family*, c.1620

104   Their Lord they shall praise,
          Their language they shall keep,
          Their land they shall lose
          Except wild Wales.*

Anonymous, of the Britons, once attributed to Taliesin,
quoted by John Davies in *Antiquae Linguae Britannicae,*1621

105   It is impossible to believe that God would have seen fit to keep this language until these days, after so many crises in the history of the nation . . .   had he not intended His name to be called and His great works to be proclaimed in it.*

106   The Britons called themselves . . . *Cymry*, that is, the original inhabitants, and they called their language *Cymraeg*, the original or innate speech, not because they believed that the nation and the language sprang from the earth like a toadstool, but because the beginnings of the nation and the language were older than anyone could remember.*

107   Wales is fading, the bards are in their graves.*

Anonymous poet, 1627

108   O blood-red Brythons, take the labour and trouble to set out your rich speech, unless you are of the same opinion as the anglicized Welsh, who believe it is better that our language should be annihilated and exterminated so that this whole island should speak the language of the English.*

Rowland Vaughan, *Yr Ymarfer o Dduwioldeb*, 1630

109   There were three jovial Welshmen,
          As I have heard men say,
    And they would go a-hunting, boys,
          Upon St David's Day;
    And all the day they hunted,
          But nothing could they find
    Except a ship a-sailing,
          A-sailing with the wind.

English ballad, *c*.1632

110   A noble peer of mickle trust and power
    Has in his charge, with tempered awe to guide
    An old and haughty nation proud in arms.

John Milton, of the Earl of Bridgewater
and his lands in Wales, *Comus*, 1634

111   Among all the countries of the world, there is no nation more lacking in love and more hostile to its own language than the Welsh, although our language, because of its antiquity and richness, deserves as much respect as any other language.*

John Edwards, *Madruddyn y Difinyddeaeth Diweddaraf*, 1652

112   The English, who formerly were ravenous wolves, have for us become cherishing shepherds.*

Charles Edwards, *Y Ffydd Ddi-ffuant*, 1667

113   'Tis to the Welsh a foul disgrace
          That in religion they are so young
    That not a tenth of all the race
          The Scriptures read in their own tongue.*

Rhys Prichard, *Canwyll y Cymru*, 1681

114   The land is mountainous and yields pretty handsome clambering for goats, and hath variety of precipices to break one's neck, which a man must do sooner than fill his belly, the soil being barren and an excellent place to breed famine in.

William Richards, *Wallography*, 1682

115   Their native gibberish is usually prattled throughout the whole of Taphydom except in their market towns, whose inhabitants, being a little raised . . . do begin to despise it. 'Tis usually cashiered out of gentlemen's houses . . . so that, if the stars prove lucky, there may be some glimmering hopes that the British language may be quite extinct and may be English'd out of Wales.

116   And thus it pleased the Almighty to deal with us the Britons; for these many ages have eclipsed our power and corrupted our language and almost blotted us out of the Books of Records.

Thomas Jones, *The British Language in its Lustre*, 1688

117   The guile and softness of the Saxon race
      In gallant Briton's soul had never place;
      Strong as his rocks and in his language pure,
      In his own innocence and truth secure:
      Such is the bold, the noble mountaineer,
      As void of treason as he is of fear.

The Brogyntin Poet, 'On the Welsh', *c*.1690

118   A Welch woman? Prithee, of what country's that?

Aesop to Quaint

      That, Sir, is a country in the world's backside where every man is born a gentleman, and a genealogist.

Quaint to Aesop, John Vanbrugh, *Aesop*, 1697

119   The fag end of Creation; the very rubbish of Noah's flood; the highest English hills are as cherrystones to the Welsh Alps, so that there is not in the whole world a people that live so near to and yet so far from heaven, as the Welsh do.

E.B., *A Trip to North Wales*, 1700

120   The language is inarticulate and guttural and sounds more like the gobbling of geese or turkeys than the speech of rational creatures.

121   Nothing can be imagined so troublesome as a Welshman possessed with the spirit of genealogy.

122   There is, I believe, no part of the Nation more inclined to be religious, and to be delighted with it, than the poor inhabitants of these Mountains.

Erasmus Saunders, *View of Religion in the Diocese of St David's*, 1721

123   The Devil lives in the middle of Wales.
      Daniel Defoe, *Tour through the Whole Island of Great Britain*, 1724

124   They [the Welsh] value themselves much on their antiquity, the ancient race of their houses, families and the like, and above all, their ancient heroes . . . and, as they believe their country to be the pleasantest and most agreeable in the world, so you cannot oblige them more than to make them think that you believe so too.

125   Its misfortune is that it is not at all known in foreign countries, unless in a small province of France [Brittany]; and very little known in this our own island, the principality of Wales excepted. Yet herein the language as well as its proprietors did but share in the common fate of all conquered nations; for it is very obvious that the language of such must as well give way to the language of the conquerors, as the necks of the inhabitants must truckle under the yokes of their subduers.
      William Gambold, in preface to his *Welsh Grammar*, 1727

126   Cambria, my darling scene!
      Richard Savage, 'To John Powell', 1730

127   It has been the continual blind complaint of some uneasy men . . . that the preserving of Welsh . . . is keeping up a discord between the subjects of the Monarchs of Great Britain; if so, God forbid we should ever talk Welsh . . . But amity and concord among men does not consist in the Language they speak . . . but in the congruity of their opinions in Religion and Politics.
      Lewis Morris, in letter to his brother William, April 1736

128   I have seen no part of England so pleasant for sixty or seventy miles together as those parts of Wales I have been in. And most of the inhabitants are indeed ripe for the Gospel. I mean . . . they are earnestly desirous of being instructed in it, and as utterly ignorant of it they are as any Creek or Cherokee Indians.
      John Wesley, entry in journal, 20 October 1739

129   She [the Welsh language] has not lost her charms, her chasteness, remains unalterably the same . . . she still retains the beauties of her youth, grown old in years, but not decayed. I pray that due regard may be had to her great age, her intrinsic usefulness, and that her longstanding repute may not be stained by wrong imputations . . . Let her stay the appointed time to expire a peaceful and natural death, which we trust will not be till the

consummation of all things, when all the languages of the world will be reduced into one again.

Griffith Jones, in Welch Piety, 1740

130   In all cases where the kingdom of England, or that part of Great Britain called England, hath been or shall be mentioned in any Act of Parliament, the same has been and shall from henceforth be deemed and taken to comprehend and include the Dominion of Wales.

Act of Parliament, 1746

131   'Tis a tongue (it seems) not made for any mouth; as appears by an instance of one in our company who, having got a Welsh polysyllable into his throat, was almost choked with consonants, had we not, by clapping him on the back, made him disgorge a guttural or two, and so saved him.

John Torbuck, A Collection of Welsh Travels
and Memoirs of Wales, 1749

132   Perhaps it were to be wished that the rules of poetry in our language were less nice and accurate; we should then undoubtedly have more writers, but perhaps fewer good ones . . . As English poetry is too loose, so ours is certainly too much confined and limited.

Goronwy Owen, in letter to Richard Morris, 21 February 1753

133   Yet our name hath not been quite blotted out from under Heaven. We hitherto not only enjoy the true name of our Ancestors but have preserved entire and uncorrupted . . . that primitive language, spoken as well by the ancient Gauls and Britons some thousands of years ago.

Thomas Richards, Thesaurus, 1753

134   Our bishops look upon me . . . with an evil eye because I dare to have any affection for my country, language and antiquities, which in their opinion had better been lost and forgotten.*

Evan Evans (Ieuan Brydydd Hir),
in letter to Lewis Morris, 12 May 1764

135   To be a passive and unconcerned spectator of . . . the extirpation of the language of one's ancestors betrays a tameness of spirit and a servility of disposition by no means becoming a gentleman, or one that hath any ancestry to boast of.

John Walters, A Dissertation on the Welsh Language, 1771

136   The false historians of a polished age
         Show that the Saxon has not lost his rage.
         Though tamed by arts, his rancour still remains:
         Beware of Saxons still, ye Cambrian swains.
         Evan Evans (Ieuan Brydydd Hir), 'The Love of our Country', 1772

137   As for our countrymen who are too apt to neglect and forget
their mother-tongue, it is to be hoped it is more out of ignorance
and affectation than hatred and ill-will.
         Rhys Jones, in preface to *Gorchestion Beirdd Cymru*, 1773

138   Why, Cambria, did I quit thy shore,
            The scenes I loved so dear?
         With wounded feelings rankling sore
            I languish, and thy loss deplore
         In Folly's hateful sphere.
    Edward Williams (Iolo Morganwg), 'Stanzas written in London', 1773

139   Wales is so little different from England that it offers
nothing to the speculation of the traveller.
         Samuel Johnson, in letter to James Boswell, 1774

140   From that moment, as by a charm the tumults subsided;
obedience was restored; peace, order and civilization followed in
the train of liberty. When the day star of the English constitution
had risen in their hearts, all was harmony within and without.
         Edmund Burke, on the Act of Union of 1536, in speech in
                                 the House of Commons, 22 March 1775

141   To the gluttonous great ones of our iand
         Corruption came from England.*
                             Evan Evans (Ieuan Brydydd Hir), elegy for
                                 William Vaughan of Corsygedol, 1775

142   At Pembroke in the evening we had the most elegant
congregation I have seen since we came into Wales. Some of them
came in dancing and laughing as into a theatre, but their mood
was quickly changed and in a few minutes they were as serious as
my subject – Death.
         John Wesley, entry in journal, 19 July 1777

143   The season of the Welsh poetry has long since been over and
so I trust that the attempt will never be revived.
         Thomas Pennant, in letter to the Revd John Lloyd, January 1778

144   Taffy was a Welshman,
      Taffy was a thief,
   Taffy came to my house
      And stole a leg of beef.

   I went to Taffy's house,
      Taffy was in bed,
   I picked up a poker
      And hit him on the head.

traditional English rhyme, c.1780

145   There were very few castles in North Wales before its conquest by the English.

Thomas Pennant, *Tours in Wales*, 1781

146   We have no coal exported from this port [Cardiff], nor ever shall, as it would be too expensive to bring it down here from the internal part of the country.

customs officer, 1782

147   At this very time, woollens instead of linen prevail among the poorer Welsh, who are subject to foul eruptions.

Gilbert White, *The Natural History of Selborne*, 1788

148   If Milton was right when he called Liberty a mountain nymph, I am now writing to you from her residence; and the peaks of our Welsh Alps heighten the idea, by wearing the clouds of heaven like a cap of Liberty.

Evan Lloyd, in letter to John Wilkes, 1790

149   This being the day on which the autumnal equinox occurred, some Welsh bards, resident in London, assembled in congress on Primrose Hill, according to ancient usage.

Anonymous, in *The Gentleman's Magazine*, October 1792

150   At Bala is nothing remarkable except a lake of eleven miles in circumference.

Samuel Taylor Coleridge, in letter to Robert Southey, 15 July 1794

151   Pistyll Rhaeadr and Wrexham steeple,
      Snowdon's mountain without its people,
      Overton's yew-trees, St Winifred's wells,
      Llangollen's bridge and Gresford's bells.

'The Seven Wonders of North Wales', late eighteenth century

152   A vast treasure is contained in the Welsh language, in manuscripts and the oral traditions of the people, of which barely a notice has hitherto been given to the world.

Anonymous, in *The Cambrian Register*, 1796

153   The manners of Wales still border on intemperance; though it be not an indispensable duty of hospitality, as it has been, to drench the guest into insensibility, indisposition or death.

David Williams, *History of Monmouthshire*, 1796

154   The history of Wales is a calendar of usurpations, depredations, and murders.

Henry Penruddocke Wyndham, *A Gentleman's Tour through Monmouthshire and Wales,* 1797

155   I have since seen, in the most retired spots of this country, a wretched cottage nearly bursting with the fullness of its congregation; and multitudes, in a heavy rain, swarming about the outside, imbibing, with gasping mouths, the poisonous tenets of a mechanical preacher.

156   Cardiff is a populous but ill-built town, nor is there any thing very pleasing in its environs.

157   I don't recollect to have seen one beggar before in the whole tour; the common people were indeed poor enough, but they seemed contented with their lot, and were always willing to answer our enquiries, without the least expectation of reward; they never asked for it; and when we sometimes gave the half-clothed wretch a shilling, they received it with an awkward surprise, and were so astonished that they could only express their thanks in tears of gratitude.

158   I have seen groups of poor people in the sequestered spots of both North and South Wales ... at the sight of an unexpected man of the world, they will run into a rocky cavity, like a rabbit into its hole, or plunge into the thickest shade as if they were escaping from a beast of prey.

Samuel Jackson Pratt, *Gleanings through Wales, Holland and Westphalia*, 1798

159   How oft, in spirit, have I turned to thee,
    O sylvan Wye! thou wanderer through the woods,
    How often has my spirit turned to thee!

Wordsworth, 'Lines composed a few miles above Tintern Abbey', 1798

160   If, therefore, in the colloquial intercourse of the scholars, one of them be detected in speaking a Welsh word, he is immediately degraded with the 'Welsh lump', a large piece of lead fastened to a string, and suspended round the neck of the offender. The mark of ignominy has had the desired effect: all the children of Flintshire speak English very well.

Richard Warner, A Second Walk through Wales, 1799

161   In Walbrook stands a famous inn,
            Near ancient Watling Street,
      Well stored with brandy, beer and gin,
            Where Cambrians nightly meet.

      If on the left you leave the bar
            Where the Welsh landlord sits,
      You'll find the room where wordy war
            Is waged by Cambrian wits.

David Samwell, 'The Padouca Hunt', 1799

162   North Wales is now as Methodistical as south Wales, and south Wales as Hell.

Edward Williams (Iolo Morganwg), in letter to
Owen Jones (Owain Myfyr), 1799

163   The inhabitants [of western Monmouthshire] unwillingly hold intercourse with the English, retain their ancient prejudices and still brand them with the name of Saxons.

William Coxe, An Historical Tour through Monmouthshire, 1801

164   The sudden decline of the national minstrelsy and customs of Wales is in a great degree to be attributed to the fanatick imposters, or illiterate plebian preachers, who have too often been suffered to over-run the country, misleading the greater part of the common people from their lawful church, and dissuading them from their innocent amusements, such as singing, dancing, and other rural sports, with which they had been accustomed to delight in from earliest times . . . The consequence is, Wales, which was formerly one of the merriest and happiest countries in the world, is now become one of the dullest.

Edward Jones, in preface to The Bardic Museum, 1802

165   Every one feels that partiality for his native country so distinctly working in his breast, as to require no kind of argument for its existence; but it probably assumes a more active sway over

the mind of a people whom the revolutions of the world have deprived of independency, and whose name appears on the verge of oblivion among the nations, who in their turn are rising into pre-eminence.

William Owen Pughe, introduction to
A Welsh and English Dictionary, 1803

166   The Welsh language lays claim to high antiquity, as being a branch of the Jaspian, or that dialect of the Hebrew spoken by the prosperity of Japhet.

John Evans, *Letters written during a
Tour through North Wales in the Year 1798*, 1804

167   On the whole, the pleasure of a tour in Wales is in some degree tinged with melancholy, on observing the honest and amiable manners of its inhabitants, to find so many appearances of a fallen country.

Benjamin Heath Malkin, *The Scenery, Antiquity,
and Biography of South Wales*, 1804

168   North Wales is becoming English.

169   Radnorshire is generally considered, in a picturesque point of view, as the least interesting of the Welsh counties.

170   The language of Radnorshire is almost universally English. In learning to converse with their Saxon neighbours, they have forgotten the use of their vernacular language.

171   The workmen of all descriptions at these immense works [at Cyfarthfa, Merthyr Tydfil] are Welshmen. Their language is entirely Welsh. The number of English amongst them is very inconsiderable.

172   It is very remarkable that great immoralities do not prevail in any part of Wales, not even in places contiguous to large manufactories, especially if the English language happens to be but little spoken.

173   Almost all the Welsh sects among the lower orders of the people have in truth degenerated into habits of the most pitiable lunacy in their devotion. The various subdivisions of methodists, jumpers and I know not what, who meet in fields and houses, prove how low fanaticism may degrade human reason.

174   The greatest fault imputed to the common people by their superiors is the want of a due regard to their own interests, without which they are never likely to be industrious, though they may be faithful servants to their employers.

175   Wales yields not, in the shadow of a thought, to England, in loyalty to the reigning family. Indeed, the King seems to be the only Saxon to whom they are thoroughly reconciled.

176   The treachery of the Saxons, whom the original Britons introduced into the island as friends and allies, and their cruelty in exterminating in cold blood the nobility of the ancient inhabitants . . . still rankles in the bosoms of the indigenous sons of freedom.
Theophilus Evans, *The History of Brecknockshire*, 1805

177   The Welch antiquaries have considerably injured their very high claims to confidence by attempting to detail very remote events with all the accuracy belonging to the facts of yesterday. You will have one of them describe you the cut of Llywarch Hen's beard or the whittle of Urien Rheged with as much authority as if he had trimmed the one or cut his cheese with the other. These high pretensions weaken greatly our belief in the Welch poems, which probably contain great treasure.
Sir Walter Scott, in letter to a friend, 1805

178   Oh beauteous Meirion! Cambria's mountain-pride!
Thomas Love Peacock, *The Philosophy of Melancholy*, 1812

179   Steal, if possible, my revered friend, one summer from the cold hurry of business, and come to Wales.
Percy Bysshe Shelley, in letter to William Godwin,
25 April 1812

180   The society in Wales is very stupid. They are all aristocrats and Christians but as to that I tell you I do not mind in the least: the unpleasant part of the business is that they hunt people to death who are not so likewise.
in letter to James Hogg, December 1812

181   The Rhondda is the wildest region of Glamorganshire, where the English language is scarce ever heard.
J. G. Wood, *The Principal Rivers of Wales*, 1813

182   Among the peasantry of North Wales, the ancient

mountains, with all their terrors and all their glories, are pictures to the blind, and music to the deaf.

Samuel Taylor Coleridge, *Biographia Literaria*, 1817

183   The building appeared to be a school and the children were chanting a Welch psalm. I never heard sounds that charmed me as these did. Never did music give me such pleasure before. I regretted the moment when they ceased to vibrate and left us to sink down into common life again.

Michael Faraday, *Journal of a Walking Tour through Wales*, 1819

184   Three tries for a Welshman.*

traditional saying, *c.*1820

185   Three jolly Welshmen coming out of Wales,
Riding on a nanny-goat, selling sheeps' tails.

traditional children's rhyme, Salop, *c.*1820

186   We, who are natives and the real owners, cannot stretch a foot without being trod on.

protest of Tredegar workers against 'the children of
Hengist and Horsa' (the English masters), *c.*1820

187   There has been riot and commotion in England, Scotland and Ireland, because [those countries] neither feared God nor honoured the King . . . but our nation remained wonderfully faithful to the Government in all its troubles.

Robert Jones, *Drych yr Amseroedd*, 1820

188   You hear the Welsh spoken much about you, and if you can pick it up without interfering with more important labours, it will be worth while.

Sir Walter Scott, in letter to his son Charles,
19 December 1820

189   All trades and professions here are in the most delightful confusion. The druggist sells hats and the shoemaker is the sole bookseller, if that dignity can be allowed him on the strength of the three Welsh Bibles and the Guide to Caernarvon which adorn his window. The grocer sells ropes and the clothes brush is a luxury as yet unknown in Llanrwst.

Lord Macaulay, in letter to his mother, 1821

190   Wales, as is pretty well known, breeds a population some-
what litigious.
Thomas de Quincey, Confessions of an English Opium-Eater, 1822

191   While the national peculiarities, whether in manners or
literature, of Scotland and Ireland, have been industriously
explored, and in many instances successfully developed, Wales has
been regarded with an indifference not easily to be reconciled with
that spirit of enterprise by which the literary public of Great
Britain is known to be animated.
John Humphreys Parry, The Cambrian Plutarch, 1824

192   The general pursuit of the Welsh is agriculture; but without
approximation to excellence, for the cattle are subjected to
privations and the soil to ingratitude.
John Jones, A History of Wales, 1827

193   How mad the dull mysticism, how atrocious the gloomy
passion, of Wales must seem amid the lucid common sense and
unimpassioned judgement of England, may easily be conceived.
Anonymous, in Blackwood's Magazine, November 1829

194   Here I am in Wales . . . and a harper sits in the vestibule of
every inn and never stops playing so-called folk-melodies, that is,
infamous, common, faked stuff.*
Felix Mendelssohn, in letter to Carl Friedrich Zelter, 1829

195   Only two things can save a cornered hare – God and a
Cardiganshire jury.
traditional saying, c.1830

196   During centuries this country was the theatre for the display
of the most heroic courage and conspicuous martial prowess ever
exhibited to the world.
Henry Gastineau, Wales Illustrated, 1830

197   Wales, whether considered with reference to the nature of
the country, its picturesque scenery, geographical features, or rare
productions, independent of its history, as a people whose
circumstances, actions, and fate, stand single and unparalleled in
the annals of the world, possesses peculiar interest, and is of the
highest importance.

198   I saw the Merthyr riots,
And the great oppression of the workers;
Sixty were killed outright
And some of the soldiers wounded . . .
But dear heaven! the worst trick
Was the hanging of Dic Penderyn.*

                                               ballad, 1831

199   There has been a great riot in Wales and the soldiers have killed twenty-four people. When two or three were killed at Manchester, it was called the Peterloo Massacre and the newspapers for weeks wrote it up as the most outrageous and wicked proceeding ever heard of. But that was in Tory times; now this Welsh riot is scarcely mentioned.

                       Mrs Arbuthnot, entry in diary, June 1831

200   In these days of sedition and threatened anarchy, the Principality has always been tranquil and happy as Goschen.

        John Blackwell (Alun), in address to the Beaumaris Eisteddfod, 1832

201   My thoughts, wild Cambria, dwell with thee!

            Felicia Dorothea Hemans, 'The Cambrian in America', 1832

202   The chapel preachers never lead the people except at funerals.

              Dr William Price, in speech at Llantrisant, c.1832

203   Merthyr Tydfil is remarkable for the number and extent of its iron-works, the whole of the surrounding district, eight miles in length and four in breadth, abounding in iron and coals. Scarcely anything can be conceived more awfully grand than the descent, on a dark night, into the Vale of Merthyr Tydfil, from any of the surrounding hills, where on a sudden the traveller beholds, as it were, numberless volcanoes breathing out their undulating pillars of flame and smoke.

        M. A. Leigh, *Guide to Wales and Monmouthshire*, 1833

204   The Celt is ever ready to revolt against the despotism of fact.*

                Henri Martin, *Histoire de France*, 1833

205   The continuance of the [Welsh] language is of no benefit to the country; it is kept up . . . to keep the dissenters together.

      E. P. Richards, in letter to the Marquess of Bute, 11 December 1833

206   The bishop's address . . . turned chiefly on reproof of
Dissenters, who, to our shame, have done more for religion in
Wales than our Church has ever attempted.

> Lady Charlotte Guest, entry in journal, 6 October 1834

207   Samaria? What was Samaria? Samaria was their ash-tip. An
ash-tip where they threw all their sticks and rubbish. A hot-bed of
Paganism and Heresy and everything. Yes, my friends, Samaria
was the Merthyr Tydfil of the Land of Canaan.*

> David Rowland, in sermon *c*.1835

208   The Tory landlords brought their Tenants up themselves like
flocks of sheep and made them break their pledge-words. They
absolutely dragged them to the Poll, threatening to turn them out
of their farms unless they voted plumpers for Lord Adare.

> Lady Charlotte Guest, entry in journal, 4 August 1837

209   We all went to the Cymreigyddion Meeting which was
brilliantly attended . . . But it seemed to me that there was not the
same display of genuine and native enthusiasm among the lower
order of Welsh Literati themselves, which had been so animating
and gratifying in 1835. I am afraid the Society is beginning to be
tamed down to the conventional rules of English taste.

> entry in journal, 18 October 1837

210   My dear children, Infants as you yet are, I feel that I cannot
dedicate more fitly than to you these venerable relics of ancient
lore, and I do so in the hope of inciting you to cultivate the
Literature of 'Gwyllt Gwalia' [Wild Wales], in whose beautiful
language you are being initiated, and amongst whose free
mountains you were born. May you become early imbued with the
chivalric and exalted sense of honour and the fervent patriotism
for which its sons have ever been celebrated.

> dedication 'to Ivor and Merthyr' of her translation
> of the Mabinogion, 1838

211   A wild and mountainous region where nature seemed to
reign in stern and unbroken silence.

> Thomas Roscoe, of the Rhondda valleys,
> *Wanderings through South Wales,* 1838

212   Within the stones of Federation there,
  On the green turf, and under the blue sky,
  A noble band, the Bards of Britain stood,

Their heads in reverence bare, and bare of foot,
A deathless brotherhood!

Robert Southey, 'The Gorsedd', 1838

213   It is true that others have made Wales the scene of action for the heroes of their tales; but however talented such works might be, to the Welshman's feeling they lacked nationality, and betrayed the hand of the foreigner in the working of the web.

Thomas Jeffery Llewelyn Prichard, in preface to
The Adventures and Vagaries of Twm Shon Catti (2nd edn, 1839)

214   It is remarkable how fluently little boys and girls can speak Welsh.

Alfred, Lord Tennyson, in letter to Emily Sellwood, 1839

215   I cannot say I have seen much worth the trouble of the journey, excepting the Welsh women's hats, which look very comical to the English eye, being in truth men's beaver-hats, with the brim a little broad and tied under the chin with a black ribbon. Some faces look very pretty in them.

216   I could not help thinking of the defensible nature of the country in the case of foreign invasion! A few thousand of armed men on the hills could successfully defend them. Wales would make an excellent Republic.

Henry Vincent, in *The Western Vindicator*, 6 April 1839

217   Wales is divided into 844 parishes, in which there are about 1,000 churches and chapels.

William Jones, *The Character of the Welsh as a Nation*
in the Present Age, 1841

218   Never has the Welsh language been more encouraged than during the last twenty-five years, and never, in the same compass of time, has the English spread itself so much over the principality.

219   On the whole I am inclined to the opinion that the extinction of the language is impracticable; consequently, the discouragement of it must be both impolitic and wicked.

220   I fear the opinion held by many is true, that not twenty females in Wales are acquainted with the grammar of their native tongue.

221   A strong feeling of prejudice is entertained by each religious party against all the others which co-exist.

222   While adultery is a crime seldom heard of, instances in which parties preparing for marriage forestall the privileges of that sacred state are shamefully numerous.

223   To exist after so many and persevering attempts at their extinction, and to retain the vernacular use of their primitive, nervous, and enchanting language, after so many revolutions in their civil and religious circumstances, are facts in which they will forever glory; and no good reason appears why our English neighbours should deny us the consolation of these facts, or laugh at us, with so much sarcastic malevolence, when the matter is discussed in their society.

224   Merthyr, the Gehenna of Wales, where black beings dwell, amidst fire and smoke, who dive into deep caverns, where opportunities are afforded them to concoct their treasonable designs against the inhabitants of the upper world.

225   But for their dissensions and questionable views of politics, the Independents would have much that would be deserving of commendation.

226   There is a large number of good people among them [the Baptists], and were it not for the tendency of their system to general anarchy, they would not be an uninteresting portion of society.

227   The Methodists of the Wesleyan Persuasion are not a very numerous body of people in Wales.

228   It is devoutly to be wished that the [Anglican] clergy of Wales were more vernacularly acquainted with the language in which they officiate.

229   The people of the South are fond of conversation, and are even garrulous; one of them will talk as much in five minutes as a Northwalian will in fifteen, especially when he is a little excited.

230   In Merionethshire there is much innocence and simplicity, and the inhabitants stand pre-eminent among their countrymen for their chastity.

231 The poor of Wales are not to be considered an abandoned race of people. Some of them undoubtedly are very immoral; but many may be found who are quiet, resigned, and devoted to religion; and Christianity appears to be producing its benign and transforming influence on their minds.

232 It should be borne in mind that the animated and popular style of preaching used by Dissenters has been one of the chief means by which the people have been withdrawn from the Church; and if ever they are expected to return, it can only be achieved by that most important ordinance of the Almighty, the preaching of His truths in such a way as to tell on the heart of the audience.

233 I know not on the face of the earth a region more beautiful, more blissful, and all in all more desirable than the land of Wales.*
Thomas Price (Carnhuanawc), *Hanes Cymru*, 1842

234 The people, the masses, to a man throughout the three counties of Carmarthen, Cardigan and Pembroke are with me. O yes, they are all my children . . . Surely, say I, these are members of my family, these are the oppressed sons and daughters of Rebecca.
the Daughters of Rebecca, reported in *The Welshman*,
1 September 1843

235 The landlords are most of them of the old Church and King school. The tenantry are almost all Dissenters, with a spice of the fanaticism of the Covenanters about them.
William Day, in letter to George Cornewall Lewis, 9 July 1843

236 The people's ignorance of the English language practically prevents the working of the laws and institutions and impedes the administration of justice.
report of the Commissioners of Inquiry for South Wales, 1844

237 The Welsh Members of Parliament should resolve themselves into a united Welsh party.*
William Rees (Gwilym Hiraethog), in *Yr Amserau*, 26 March 1846

238 The people of that country labour under a peculiar difficulty from the existence of an ancient language . . . If the Welsh had the same advantages as the Scotch, they would, instead of appearing as a distinct people, in no respect differ from the English. Would it not, then, be wisdom and sound policy to send the English

schoolmaster among them . . . A band of efficient schoolmasters is
kept up at much less expense than a body of police or soldiery.

William Williams, MP for Coventry, in speech in the
House of Commons, 10 March 1846

239   The Welsh language is a vast drawback to Wales, and a
manifold barrier to the moral progress and commercial prosperity
of the people. It is not easy to over-estimate its evil effects.

Report on the State of Education in Wales,
'The Blue Books', 1847

240   The Welsh language is peculiarly evasive, which originates
from its having been the language of slavery.

Edward Lloyd Hall, in evidence

241   Perjury is common in courts of justice, and the Welsh
language facilitates it.

clerk to the magistrates at Lampeter, in evidence

242   From my experience of Ireland, I think there is a very great
similarity between the lower orders of Welsh and Irish – both are
dirty, indolent, bigoted and contented.

the curate of St Mary's, Brecon, in evidence

243   In the works the Welsh workman never finds his way into
the office . . . His language keeps him under the hatches, being one
in which he can neither acquire or communicate the necessary
information.

244   I assert with confidence, as an undeniable fact, that
fornication is not regarded as a vice, scarcely as a frailty, by the
common people in Wales. It is considered as a matter of course –
as the regular conventional progress towards marriage.

the chaplain of the Bishop of Bangor, in evidence

245   The want of chastity is the besetting evil of this country . . .
The parents do not see the evil in it. They say their daughters have
been 'unfortunate' and maintain their illegitimate grand-children
as if they were legitimate.

the vicar of Deneio, in evidence

246   The Welsh are peculiarly exempt from the guilt of great
crimes. There are few districts in Europe where murders,
burglaries, personal violence, rapes, forgeries or any felonies on a

large scale are so rare. On the other hand, there are perhaps fewer countries where the standard of minor morals is lower.

247   I regard the degraded condition [of the people of Monmouthshire] as entirely the fault of their employers, who give them far less tendance and care than they bestow on their cattle, and who with few exceptions, use and regard them as so much brute force instrumental to wealth, but as no wise involving claims on human sympathy.

248   The masters are looked upon generally as the natural enemies of the men; the intimate relation between capital and labour, and the identical interest which links their fate, are neither understood nor believed; both classes imagine that they are necessarily antagonistic.

249   These hills are of the carboniferous group and will no doubt ultimately be invaded, and perforated with coal levels. We trust that it may not happen in our day
Charles Frederick Cliffe, *The Book of South Wales*, 1847

250   The people of this solitudinous and happy valley [the Rhondda] are a pastoral race, almost wholly dependent on their flocks and herds for support . . . The air is aromatic with wild flowers and mountain plants, a sabbath stillness reigns.

251   We have raised a periodical Welsh literature for ourselves, in the course of forty years, which circulates about 60,000 copies monthly.
Evan Jones (Ieuan Gwynedd), *A Vindication of the Educational and Moral Condition of Wales*, 1848

252   By settling together [in the USA], we shall be far happier than being scattered as we are now; we should have a better ministry and our nation would be saved from extinction.*
Michael D. Jones, in *Y Cenhadwr Americanaidd*, January 1849

253   Welsh should be taught in Wales as well as English.
Queen Victoria, in letter to Lord Lansdowne, 1849

254   Ah me! 'Tis like a vision of Hell, and will never leave me, that of these poor creatures broiling, or in sweat and dirt, amid their furnaces, pits and rolling mills. For here is absolutely no aristocracy or guiding class; nothing but one or two huge iron masters, and the

rest are operatives, petty shopkeepers, Scottish hawkers. The town [Merthyr Tydfil] might be, and will be, one of the prettiest places in the world. It *is* one of the sootiest, squalidest, and ugliest; all cinders and dust-mounds and soot.

> Thomas Carlyle, in letter to his wife, August 1850

255 Mothers of Wales, speak Welsh to your children . . . It is from you, and not from their fathers, that they will learn to love God in their own language.*

> Lady Llanover, in *Y Gymraes*, vol. 1, 1850

256 For all intents and purposes of civic government, Merthyr Tydfil is as destitute as the smallest rural village in the Empire.

> T. W. Rammell, in report to the Board of Health, 1850

257 Who list to read the deeds by valiant Welshmen done,
Shall find them worthy men of arms as breathes beneath the sun;
They are of valiant hearts, of nature kind and meek,
An honour on St David's Day it is to wear the leek.

> Anonymous, reprinted 1851 from an earlier black-letter
> broadside, 'The Praise of St David's Day'

258 I consider the Welsh language a serious evil, a great obstruction to the moral and intellectual progress of my countrymen.

> Henry Austin Bruce, Lord Aberdare, in speech, 1851

259 The Rebecca Riots are a very creditable portion of Welsh History.

> Thomas Frankland Lewis, in conversation with Nassau Senior, 1852,
> quoted in David Williams, *The Rebecca Riots*, 1955

260 The name of John Jones is in Wales a perpetual incognito.

> report of the Registrar General, 1853

261 Cardiff is gaining a world-wide reputation as one of the most immoral of seaports.

> Anonymous, in *The Merthyr Guardian*, 8 January 1853

262 Wales is strictly and emphatically independent . . . Victoria is peculiarly our own Queen – Boadicea rediviva – our Buddug the Second . . . We can address our English friends, We have more

right in Victoria than thee, a larger quantity of Celtic than of Saxon blood flowing through her royal veins.

John Williams (Ab Ithel), in speech at the
Abergavenny Eisteddfod, 1853

263   At Bangor we went to a handsome hotel and hired a carriage and two horses for some Welsh place, the name of which I forget; neither can I remember a single name of any of the places through which we posted on that day, nor could I spell them if I heard them pronounced, nor pronounce if I saw them spelt.

Nathaniel Hawthorne, *Note Book*, 1854

264   It seems to me that for a man to study the early British History of our land without Welsh is, as it were, to dig the earth with a sharp stick instead of a spade.

William Barnes, 'Ancient Britons', 1856

265   The old land of my fathers is dear to me,
        Land of poets and singers, men of renown;
    Her brave warriors, patriots most excellent,
        Spilt their blood for freedom.

    My country, my country!
    I stand up for my country:
    While the sea is a wall to the well-loved place
    O! long may the old language survive.*

Evan James, 'Hen Wlad fy Nhadau', 1856

266   Our national weakness is our servility, but in a Welsh Colony we can be imbued with a new spirit.*

Michael D. Jones, in speech at Bala, 15 August 1856

267   And they went up Snowdon, too, and saw little beside fifty fog-blinded tourists, five-and-twenty dripping ponies, and five hundred empty porter bottles; wherefrom they returned, as do many, disgusted, and with great colds in their heads.

Charles Kingsley, *Two Years Ago*, 1857

268   Gentlemen, I am a Welshman, and I love my country . . . How is the renovation of the Welsh race to be brought about? By the promotion of railways. I, for one, am not ashamed to say – and I say it here boldly – that I shall be delighted to see the Welsh people anglicized. I am quite sure that the way to anglicize them is by the promotion of railways and commerce among

them, and making the English and the Welsh thoroughly one people.

Enoch G. Salisbury MP, in speech at opening of the Vale of Clwyd Railway, 14 October 1858

269   Welshpool is a town of English aspect, excepting the names over the doors, and market day, when hats such as the Long Parliament wore may be seen on the heads of the women who come in from the country.

Walter White, *All Round the Wrekin*, 1860

270   Still do the great mountains stand,
And the winds above them roar.*

John Ceiriog Hughes, 'Alun Mabon', 1861

271   To the customs of old Wales
            Changes come from year to year;
      Every generation fails,
            One has gone, the next is here.
      After a lifetime tempest-tossed
            Alun Mabon is no more,
      But the language is not lost
            And the old songs yet endure.*

272   I sat silent and melancholy, till looking from the window I caught sight of a long line of hills, which I guessed to be the Welsh hills, as indeed they proved, which sight causing me to remember that I was bound for Wales, the land of the bard, made me cast all gloomy thoughts aside and glow with all the Welsh enthusiasm with which I glowed when I first started in the direction of Wales.

George Borrow, *Wild Wales*, 1862

273   All conquered people are suspicious of their conquerors. The English have forgot that they ever conquered the Welsh, but some ages will elapse before the Welsh forget that the English have conquered them.

274   The Welsh are afraid lest an Englishman should understand their language, and, by hearing their conversation, become acquainted with their private affairs, or by listening to it, pick up their language which they have no mind that he should know – and their very children sympathize with them.

275   No language has a better supply of simple words for the

narration of events than the Welsh, and simple words are the proper garb of narration, and no language abounds more with terms calculated to express the abstrusest ideas of the metaphysician. As to its sounds – I have to observe that at the will of a master it can be sublimely sonorous, terribly sharp, diabolically guttural and sibilant, and sweet and harmonious to a remarkable degree.

276   Gentility will be the ruin of the Welsh, as it has been of many things.

277   Wherever I have been in Wales, I have experienced nothing but kindness and hospitality, and when I return to my own country I will say so.

278   Wales is a bit crazed on the subject of religion.

279   Oats and Methodism! What better symbols of poverty and meanness?

280   At this time we are one whole compact people. Remember that you are all Englishmen though you are Welshmen. Depend upon it – we must consider ourselves Englishmen.
Hussey Vivian, in speech at the Swansea Eisteddfod, 1863

281   The farmer in Wales as well as the labourer must be taken to mean a person generally badly lodged and insufficiently fed and clothed.
report of medical officer to the Privy Council, 1864

282   It is our language that keeps us a distinct nation, and because of that it is reasonable that we should keep our language.*
R. J. Derfel, 'Cadwriaeth yr Iaith Gymraeg',
Traethodau ac Areithiau, 1864

283   I am a great admirer of the old Welsh language, and I have no sympathy with those who revile it. Still, I have seen enough of the world to know that the best medium to make money by is the English language. I want to advise every one of my countrymen to master it perfectly; if you are content with brown bread, you can of course remain where you are; if you wish to enjoy the luxuries of life, with white bread to boot, the only way to do so is by learning English well. I know what it is to eat both.
David Davies of Llandinam, in speech at the National
Eisteddfod, Aberystwyth, September 1865

284   Englishmen, English capital and enterprise, English customs and unhappily, English vices, are rushing in upon us like mighty irresistible torrents carrying away before them our ancient language, social habits, and even our religious customs and influence over the masses.*

Thomas Price, in speech to the
Congregational Union, 1865

285   It would be an enormous advantage to the Welsh and to the English if the Welsh language became extinct before tomorrow morning and the Welsh became absorbed into the English nation.*

Griffith Richards, in *Y Cronicl*, vol. 23, 1865

286   The Welsh language is the curse of Wales. Its prevalence and the ignorance of English have excluded, and even now exclude, the Welsh people from the civilization, the improvement, and the material prosperity of their English neighbours . . . Their antiquated and semi-barbarous language, in short, shrouds them in darkness.

editorial in *The Times*, 8 September 1866

287   The Eisteddfod is one of the most mischievous and selfish pieces of sentimentalism which could possibly be perpetrated. It is simply a foolish interference with the natural progress of civiliza- tion and prosperity. If it is desirable that the Welsh should talk English, it is monstrous folly to encourage them in a loving fondness for their old language.

288   Wales, it should be remembered, is a small country, unfavourably situated for commercial purposes, with an indifferent soil, and inhabited by an unenterprising people. It is true it possesses valuable minerals but these have been chiefly developed by English energy and for the supply of English wants. A bare existence on the most primitive food of a mountainous race is all that the Welsh could enjoy if left to themselves.

editorial, 14 September 1866

289   It is the crown of the Welsh that no other nation harbours ill feeling against them in any sense.*

editorial in *Y Gwladgarwr*,
18 August 1866

290   When I see the enthusiasm these Eisteddfods can awaken in your whole people, and then think of the tastes, the literature, the

amusements of our own lower and middle class, I am filled with admiration.

Matthew Arnold, in reply to invitation to visit the
Eisteddfod at Chester, 1866

291   On this side Wales – Wales, where the past still lives. Where every place has its tradition, every name its poetry, and where the people, the genuine people, still knows this past, this tradition, this poetry, and lives with it, and clings to it; while, alas, the prosperous Saxon on the other side, the invader from Liverpool and Birkenhead, has long forgotten his.

Matthew Arnold, *On the Study of Celtic Literature*, 1866

292   It must always be the desire of a government to render its dominions, as far as possible, homogenous . . . Sooner or later the difference of language between Wales and England will probably be effaced . . . an event which is socially and politically so desirable.

293   The practical contribution of Welsh culture to that of England and the world at large must be made in English.

294   The sooner the Welsh language disappears as an instrument of the practical, political, social life of Wales, the better; the better for England, the better for Wales itself.

295   There is no country in Europe where there are not different nationalities under the same government. The Highland Gaels and the Welsh are undoubtedly of different nationalities from the English, although nobody will give to these remnants of peoples long gone by the titles of nations any more than to the Celtic inhabitants of Brittany in France.*

Friedrich Engels, *What Have the Working Classes
to do with Poland?*, 1866

296   The literature of Wales is remarkable for the purity of its sentiments and the high tone of its morality. Infidelity or scepticism have found no room for their utterance. We have hardly a single publication among the hundred of thousands that find circulation in the Principality that can give offence to the high moral sentiments produced by our common Christianity.

John Griffiths, in speech at the Music Hall, Chester,
6 February 1866

297   Let English be the language of commerce and Welsh the language of religion.*
Thomas Gee, in *Baner ac Amserau Cymru*, 1 August 1866

298   Clansmen battling for their respective chieftains.
Henry Richard, of Welsh politicians, *Letters on the Social
and Political Condition of Wales*, 1866

299   The Welsh are cordially liked and heartily respected by all their fellow-subjects, as a gallant and most gifted race. Year by year the English know them better, and year by year the English like them more. There is really not even a lingering trace of national jealousy. Long ago, we fought our last fight with the Welsh, and luckily for them we won it.
editorial in *Daily Telegraph*, 13 September 1867

300   The Eisteddfod, with its mottoes and hieroglyphics, must be in a desperately shaky condition if it cannot stand a little of that gentle raillery to which usage has now given the appropriate name of 'chaff'.

301   Ever since the incorporation of Wales with England, the loyalty of the Welsh nation to their Saxon rulers has been perfectly unswerving, nothwithstanding the occasional effusions of frenzied poets and hot-headed orators against the Saxon invaders.
Thomas Rees, *Miscellaneous Papers on Subjects
relating to Wales*, 1867

302   Novels, the disgrace of English literature and the curse of multitudes of English readers, do not take well with Welsh readers.
Thomas Rees, in *Carmarthen Journal*, 6 September 1867

303   The Welsh are a conquered race, and have very little regard for their conquerors, and even some of the most ignorant of them are so stupid as to entertain the notion of reclaiming their country from the English.
H. L. Spring, *Lady Cambria*, 1867

304   Had the mineral wealth of the Principality been discovered by the natives, and could it have been properly put to use before they were subdued by English rule, they might have preserved their language and have been the foremost amongst British subjects in wealth, manufactures and arts; but as the English have,

through Providence, been the means of opening out her resources, it is plain that the English element must universally prevail.

305   To rouse the old land to its former glory.*
John Ceiriog Hughes, 'Cadlef Morgannwg', 1868

306   The most important and valuable of all things connected with Wales is her language.
James Kenward, *For Cambria*, 1868

307   I call upon the young men of Wales to rise energetically to meet the present emergency. Do not believe that the existence of two languages in our country is an unmixed evil, any more than that the existence of two climates or two kinds of scenery is one. You who were born and also live on Cambrian soil, be the earnest and consistent advocates of your nation's rights, the vindicators of its fame, the representatives of its genius and worth.

308   An Englishman wishing to cast in his lot with Welsh interest is distracted by the dissension everywhere present.

309   No question relating to Wales has occupied the attention of Parliament in the memory of man.
Henry Richard MP, in speech in the House of Commons, 1869

310   Wales, England – and Llanrwst.*
traditional saying, *c.*1870

311   Talk in Welsh
And sing in Welsh;
Whatever you do,
Do everything in Welsh.*
Richard Davies (Mynyddog), 'Gwnewch Bobpeth yn Gymraeg', 1870

312   Very gallant young fellows these Celts, also born dialecticians, everything is conceived in Triads.*
Karl Marx, in letter to Friedrich Engels, 11 May 1870

313   In the best interest of the Welsh it is desirable to do everything lawful to wean them from their provincial tongue. There can be no doubt its use is gradually dying out and it is permissible to hasten a process which has simultaneously arisen among the people themselves from the course of events.
editorial in *The Times*, 14 November 1871

314   Mr Marsden [the vicar of Glascwm, Rads.] told me that only four years ago died the last old woman who could speak her native Radnorshire Welsh, her northern tongue which she had learnt as a child from her mother and grandmother, never having lived out of her own parish. No one else in the parish could talk Welsh to her except Mr Marsden and her great delight was when he would read to her from a Welsh book.

Francis Kilvert, entry in diary, 22 May 1871

315   The Metropolis of Wales.

epithet for Cardiff, first used in 1873

316   Wales, sweet Wales, I believe I must have Welsh blood. I always feel so happy and natural and at home among the kindly Welsh.

Francis Kilvert, entry in diary, 12 April 1875

317   Dear motherland, forgive me, if too long
      I hold the halting tribute of my song;
      Letting my wayward fancy idly roam
      Far, far from thee, my early home.
      There are some things too near,
      Too infinitely dear
      For speech; the old ancestral hearth.
      The hills, the vales that saw our birth,
      Are hallowed deep within the reverent breast:
      And who of these keeps silence, he is best.

Sir Lewis Morris, 'To my Motherland', 1875

318   The whole mental machinery of the Welsh and Irish seems better oiled than that of the Saxon.

Anonymous, in *The Cornhill Magazine*, vol. 36, 1877

319   I speak of the country of Wales . . . There is no part that can exceed it from one end of this island to the other in the ardent, and I may say, passionate love for instruction.

William Ewart Gladstone, in speech at Nottingham, 1877

320   Lovely the woods, waters, meadows, combes, vales,
      All the air things wear that build this world of Wales;
      Only the inmate does not correspond.

Gerard Manley Hopkins, 'In the Valley of the Elwy', 1877

321   The greater part of the demand among us for English

chapels arises from the haughty pride of men made servile by adulation of the English.*

Michael D. Jones, in *Y Ddraig Goch*, June 1877

322   Few of them show intelligence. I find that when the question is translated to Welsh, they understand it better.

entry in log-book of the National School, Llanrug, Caerns.,
1 November 1878

323   It is better for a nation to be the object of English hatred than of their scorn.*

Robert Ambrose Jones (Emrys ap Iwan), 'Dr Edwards a'r
Achosion Seisnigol', in *Baner ac Amserau Cymru*, 1880

324   Oh, how we love a bit of stroking! We should rather, Mr Gladstone, be without bread than without soap. If you tickle us in a tender spot we lie still as a litter of piglets on a dungheap. We half-worship you since you called us 'patient and loyal Welshmen', and especially since you described our country as 'poor little Wales'.*

in letter to *Baner ac Amserau Cymru*, 1880

325   You, the coalowners, are the Welsh Pharaohs who think you can suck the lifeblood of the colliers for ever. You have grown fat and prosperous; you own the big houses; you wear the finest clothes; your children are healthy and happy; yet you do not work. How then have you got those things by idleness? . . . Take heed, you men whose bodies are bloated by the lifeblood of the poor, take heed before it is too late. Remember that the oppression of the Pharaohs did not last for ever, and neither will the oppression of the blood-sucking Pharaohs of Wales.

Dr William Price of Llantrisant (1800–93), quoted by Rhys Davies,
'A Drop of Dew', in *Wales*, no. 31, October 1949

326   Such is the attachment of the Welsh to their own language and literature, so deeply interwoven are they with their daily life, their religious worship and even their amusements, that . . . the Welsh language will long be cherished by the large majority of the Welsh people.

report of the Committee on Intermediate and
Higher Education in Wales, 1881

327   Where there is a distinctively formed Welsh opinion upon a given subject, which affects Wales alone . . . I know of no

reason why a respectful regard should not be paid to that opinion.

William Ewart Gladstone, in speech in the House of Commons, 1881

328 I believe it is the suppressed condition of the Welsh that is the reason why their music is so sentimental.*

Robert Ambrose Jones (Emrys ap Iwan), 'Llythyr Alltud', in
Baner ac Amserau Cymru, 13 December 1882

329 The inaccessibility of Aberystwyth [the proposed location of the University College of Wales] to the outside world must be accepted as a dispensation of Providence. Such a town deserves to be isolated.

Thomas Davies, in letter to Thomas Charles Edwards, 1884

330 The Society for the Utilization of the Welsh Language for the Better Teaching of English.

the English title of the first Cymdeithas yr Iaith Gymraeg, 1885

331 There is an effort made by certain well-meaning but ill-advised friends of Wales to bring the Welsh language to the front and make it a class subject in our elementary schools. The true and disinterested friends of the country admit that its low social and educational condition is due to the prevalence of the Welsh language. No one objects to the study of the old language but it is quite a different matter to make it a part of the curriculum of our day schools. The children of those who earn their living by manual labour attend school for the purpose of fitting themselves the more successfully to compete in the battle of life. A knowledge of Welsh can be of no possible help to them. It is in fact a positive disadvantage.

editorial in *Western Mail*, 12 May 1885

332 Wales is at present nothing more than the Highlands of England without a Highland Line; it is a geographical expression.

Basil Jones, in speech, 1886

333 The common idea of a landlord is a man who has the mouth of a hog, the teeth of a lion, the nails of a bear, the hooves of an ass, the sting of a serpent, and the greed of the grave. The landowners of our country are, in general, cruel, unreasonable, unfeeling and unpitying men . . . Many of them have been about the most presumptuous thieves that have ever breathed.*

editorial in *Baner ac Amserau Cymru*, 2 November 1887

334 I affirm that Welsh nationality is as great a reality as English nationality.

William Ewart Gladstone, in speech at Swansea, 4 June 1887

335 Wales has not told her own tale . . . It is time your representatives . . . subject to the claim of imperial patriotism, laid their Welsh heads together and considered what are the fair claims of Wales.

336 All Wales is a sea of song.*

John Ceiriog Hughes, title of poem in *Yr Oriau Olaf,* 1888

337 I am so little eager for an independent Wales that I would as soon re-establish Druidism in Anglesey as set up an independent Parliament in Caernarvon. Union with England is essential to our existence . . . but union, even the closest, does not mean that Wales is to be Anglicized.

Henry Jones, 'Some of the Social Wants of Wales', in Transactions of the Welsh National Society, 1888–9

338 I solicit your suffrages as a Welsh Nationalist.

David Randell, in election address in Gower constituency, 1888

339 For Wales see England.

Encyclopaedia Britannica, 1888

340 Of the three Celtic races which have contributed so largely to the development and prosperity of this country [the Unites States of America] . . . the Welsh, modest, unassuming, with no desire to shine or to challenge the pretensions of their brothers, with quiet industry and unaffected dignity, have worked and laboured in various fields, winning for themselves neither fame nor fortune, but a quiet safe place and secure in the respect and confidence of their fellow men . . . They mingled freely with the others and much of their race's individuality has been lost. This has always been characteristic of the Welsh.

Anonymous contributor to *New York Times*, 1889

341 Victoria and her progeny have always been cold and indifferent towards Wales and that has begotten among the people an equivalent coldness and indifference, to say the least.*

Anonymous contributor to *Y Genedl Gymreig*, 21 August 1889

342   To me the best proof of the healthy strength of Wales is the fact that it is only in literature and music that her life has been portrayed so far.*

Owen M. Edwards, *O'r Bala i Geneva*, 1889

343   Look for a moment at those districts where the language has been supplanted by English. The inhabitants have degenerated in body and mind . . . and religion is like the shadow of a shadow.

E. Pan Jones, in speech at Llanover, 1889

344   I should prefer, of the two, to see my countrymen using splendid English than poor Welsh.*

Robert Ambrose Jones (Emrys ap Iwan), 'Picio'r Gwallt yr Hanner Cymry', in *Y Geninen*, April/July 1889

345   In North Wales we measure a man from his chin up.

David Lloyd George, in speech at his adoption meeting as Liberal candidate for Caernarfon Boroughs, 3 January 1889

346   Tell the Prince of Wales how this naturally sensitive and warmhearted people feel the neglect shown them by him and his family . . . It is very wrong of him not to come here as he takes his title from this country, which is very beautiful.

Queen Victoria in letter to Sir Henry Ponsonby, 27 August 1889

347   The Welsh people are an animated, gesticulating people.

Walt Whitman, in letter to Ernest Rhys, 24 September 1889

348   Over and above all, we shall work for a legislature, elected by the manhood and womanhood of Wales, and to them responsible. It will be the symbol and cementer of our unity as a nation, our instrument in working out our social ideals and industrial welfare, the pledge of our heritage in the British Empire, the deliverer of our message and example to humanity, the rallying point of our nationality and fulfiller of our hopes.

Thomas Edward Ellis, in speech at Bala, 1890

349   I feel so sanguine that were self-government granted to Wales she would be a model to the nationalities of the earth of a people who have driven oppression from their hillsides and initiated the glorious reign of freedom, justice and truth

David Lloyd George, in speech to the South Wales Liberal Federation, February 1890

350   The current of the time is sweeping to nationalism. Wales, in throwing in her lot with Ireland in the self-government struggle, has struck a blow not only for the national rights of another Celtic country, but also for her own.

David Lloyd George, in maiden speech in the House of
Commons, 13 June 1890

351   If we are to understand the history of Wales, and to know the Welshman's soul, we have to start with the mountains.*

Owen M. Edwards, in *Cymru*, no. 1, 15 August 1891

352   I believe there is nothing that will strengthen a Welshman's character as much as knowing the history of his own country; I believe there is no better way of educating a Welshman than with his own literature; I believe that by keeping his Welshness a Welshman will be most ready to do good, and most successful and happiest and nearest to God.*

353   The Nonconformists of Wales are the people of Wales.

William Ewart Gladstone, in speech in the House of Commons, 1891

354   In 1880 Wales declared instinctively and passionately for freedom to struggling peoples and subject races. In 1886, that year of apostasies and disasters, Wales declared for Irish national freedom more decisively than did even Ireland herself. Today, Wales appeals for freedom, and we are confident that the democracy of England will give to this appeal an early, a generous, and an enthusiastic response.

T. E. Ellis, in speech at Newcastle-upon-Tyne, 1892

355   All hope of Welsh Nationalism doing anything for some time ended when Ellis grasped the Saxon gold.

Arthur Price, of T. E. Ellis's acceptance of the office of
Junior Whip, in letter to J. E. Lloyd, 1892

356   Nor have we any desire to stimulate the Welsh language by artificial means. The Welsh language is very well able to take care of itself.

David Thomas MP, in speech in the House of Commons,
February 1892

357   [The river Rhondda] contains a large proportion of human excrement, stable and pigsty manure, congealed blood, offal and entrails from the slaughterhouses, the rotten carcases of animals,

cats and dogs in various stages of decomposition, old cast-off articles of clothing and bedding, old boots, ashes, street refuse and a host of other articles. The water is perfectly black from small coal in suspension.

report of Ystradyfodwg Urban Sanitary Board, 1893

358   It is Welshmen whose minds are poor who find Welsh to be poor.*

Robert Ambrose Jones (Emrys ap Iwan), 'Cymraeg y Pregethwr', an address to students at Bala Theological College, 25 February 1893

359   The thoughtful mind sees in these people [the Welsh] many good qualities of head and heart. Their characteristics are patient, plodding and indomitable perseverance.

Marie Trevelyan, *Glimpses of Welsh Life and Character*, 1893

360   The literary activity of Wales is to be found chiefly in the Welsh-speaking districts. It is from these districts that most of its teachers come. It is in these districts that the great poets have lived. It will be one of the aims of this magazine to lay before the English-speaking Welshman the treasures of his ancestors' thoughts.

Owen M. Edwards, in *Wales*, May 1894

361   It is not race or language that has made Wales a separate country and the Welsh a peculiar people. Wales owes its separate existence to its mountains; it is to the mountains that the Welsh people owe their national characteristics.

362   The life of one Welsh miner is of greater commercial and moral value than the whole royal crowd put together, from the Royal Great Grandmamma down to the puling Royal Great Grandchild.

Keir Hardie, in *Labour Leader*, 30 June 1894

363   Yes, Home Rule for Hell! I like every man to speak up for his own country.

David Lloyd George, at a meeting in Cardiff in response to a heckler who had shouted, ' 'Ome Rule for 'Ell', 4 October 1894

364   The educated and the leisured classes have been brought up in ignorance of the Welsh language, and often with a distinct prejudice against it as a mere patois, unworthy of the respect of

an educated and cultured man. Welshmen writing in the vernacular have, therefore, only a very limited circle to appeal to.

W. Llewelyn Williams, in address to the Honourable
Society of Cymmrodorion, 1894

365 Let the Welshman have what is his, and the foreigner what is the foreigner's! In the name of reason, what is fairer?*

Robert Ambrose Jones (Emrys ap Iwan), 'Paham y Gorfu yr
Undebwyr?', in *Y Geninen*, October 1895

366 If someone says that we are a nation equal and not subjected to the English, then why have we no Parliament?*

367 The true Welshman is he who believes and professes that the most important of all political questions is that of keeping Wales Welsh in language and spirit.*

368 The Celt is Liberal in his politics because he is Conservative in his temperament.

David Lloyd George, 'National Self-Government for Wales', in
Young Wales, 1895

369 I maintain strongly that all our demands for reform, whether in Church, Land, Education, Temperance or otherwise, ought to be concentrated in one great agitation for national self-government.

in letter to Thomas Gee, 1895

370 In Wales [the Church of England] is very much what Gibraltar is to Spain, a foreign fortress placed on the territory of a jealous, proud and susceptible nation.

Lord Rosebery, in letter to Queen Victoria, January 1895

371 Wales for ever!*

traditional saying, *c.*1896

372 There are, from Swansea to Newport, thousands upon thousand of Englishmen, as true Liberals as yourselves, who will never submit to the domination of Welsh ideas.

Robert Bird, in speech at meeting of Cymru Fydd, Newport, 16
January 1896

373 Whenever Wales awakes, her religious feeling will awaken too; with Arthur comes St David, always.*

Owen M. Edwards, 'Dewi Sant', *Cartrefi Cymru*, 1896

374 The flag of morn in conqueror's state
     Enters at the English gate;
     The vanquished eve, as night prevails,
     Bleeds upon the road to Wales.

A. E. Housman, 'The Welsh Marches', 1896

375 We plead, then, that the two great languages might remain the heritage of Wales; English as the language of the secular, and Welsh as the language of the religious life, so that in all temporal affairs on the one hand and in spiritual on the other, our country might prosper.

Idrisyn Jones, 'The Moral Importance of Retaining the Welsh Language', in *Young Wales*, August 1896

376 As a people we have been winking and smiling and frowning in the dark for centuries, under the mistaken impression that the race for which the winks and smiles and frowns were particularly meant could see them.

David Davies, 'Wales and the Welsh', in *Young Wales*, vol. 3, 1897

377 There is no portion of the United Kingdom which is prouder of the British Empire than Wales. In our call for domestic self-government there is not a shadow of a desire to impair the supreme authority of this Parliament or to advance one single step along the road to separation.

Herbert Roberts MP, in speech in the House of Commons, 1898

378 The Welsh are the Irish who couldn't swim.

popular saying, early twentieth century

379 A visitor to homes in Glamorgan is asked to help himself to sugar for his tea; in Carmarthenshire he is asked whether he wants one lump or two; in Cardiganshire he is asked to give the tea another stir.

joke, early twentieth century

380 It is the duty of every true Welshman to work to free his country from the rule of strangers, and so when he has made his country free, to be able to help others to gain their liberty.

the Socialists of Llanelly Hill, Mon., *c.* 1900

381   He talked too much about . . . Wales and Eternity.*
John John Roberts, in adjudication of poem by Ben Bowen, at
Liverpool Eisteddfod, 1900

382   Wales is a land of mountains.
Owen M. Edwards, *Wales*, 1901

383   The Wales of the future must be a free Wales.*
Ben Bowen, 'Williams Pantycelyn', *Cofiant a Barddoniaeth*, 1904

384   The Welsh are so damned Welsh it sounds like affectation.
Sir Walter Raleigh (1861–1922), attributed remark, 1904

385   I would sooner go to hell than to Wales.
H. H. Asquith MP, in speech in the House of Commons, 1905

386   Wales, a hot-bed of Liberalism and Nonconformity in the
past, will become a hot-bed of Socialism and real religion in the
future.
Mrs Philip Snowden, 'Socialism in South Wales', in
Labour Leader, 27 October 1905

387   It was believed in the country that a schoolmaster could not
speak Welsh, that it was an insult to him to believe that he could.*
Owen M. Edwards, 'Ysgol y Llan', *Clych Atgof*, 1906

388   For inasmuch as God has made you a nation, keep yourselves a nation; because He took thousands of years to fashion a
language specially for your purposes, keep that language; for in
working together with God in His intentions for you, it will be
easier for you to seek and discover Him. Who knows not that God
has preserved the Welsh nation for the reason that He has special
work to be done through them in the world? There is many a small
nation which has grown influential in a short while, and many a
mighty nation brought low as it were in a day. Nations, like
human beings, have their allotted times. Let not the Welsh be
found unready when their time is at hand.*
Robert Ambrose Jones (Emrys ap Iwan), 'Y Ddysg Newydd',
Homiliau, 1906

389   Caernarvon was founded two thousand years ago as the
outpost of a great Empire – the greatest Empire that the world had
seen. It was the Bulawayo of the Roman Empire, the very extreme
of barbarism and savagery, just a fortified camp. The ruins are still

there, and little children go to a school close by. They learn a language in that school, a dead language; it is the language of that great Empire. They go out and play amongst the ruins, and they talk a language, a living one; it is the language of the conquered and the savages. Let no man despise Wales, her language or her literature. Her time will come. When the last truckload of coal reaches Cardiff, when the last black diamond is dug out of the earth of Glamorgan, there will be men then digging gems of pure brilliance from the inexhaustible mines of the literature and language of Wales.

David Lloyd George, in speech at St David's Festival dinner,
Cardiff, 1906

390 It's worth turning exile now and again
And from little Wales to go,
In order to come back to Wales
And be able to love her more.*

Eliseus Williams (Eifion Wyn), 'Y Llanw', 1906

391 Wear a leek in your cap,
And wear one in your heart.*

'Os wyt Gymro', 1906

392 The mistake often made by many people outside Wales who think of the Welsh language is that of supposing that it has no natural spontaneous life and that it is kept alive merely by a process of artificial respiration.

Edward Anwyl, 'The Welsh Language in relation to National
Life', in *Wales Today and Tomorrow*, ed. T. Stephens, 1907

393 I rejoice that the English Churches in Wales are prospering. In the inevitable recession of Welsh, in the overwhelming inrush of English, it is a matter of joy that the needs of the people are being provided for. This is, after all, the highest patriotism.

J. Glyn Davies, 'English Churches in Wales'

394 Snowdon, the most majestic of our mountains, is hideously disfigured, and its heights have been sacrilegiously converted into a bar for the sale of Bass beers.

J. Hugh Edwards, 'From the Watch-Tower'

395 I have again and again been exceedingly amazed at the suspicion and distrust with which North Walians and South Walians, among the lower classes, regard each other.

396   Until such time as our national pride is awakened, until we find self-respect, until we put aside the worship of all things alien, until we pay due respect to our own fathers, we should not dare to deserve respect from the people of other countries.*

Owen M. Edwards, 'Ty'n-y-Groes',
Tro trwy'r Gogledd, 1907

397   Our country is something alive, not a dead grave under our feet. Every hill has its story, every district its romance. Every valley is new, every hill wears its own splendour. And for a Welshman, no other country can be like this.*

'Adfyfyrion'

398   The Welsh language is not sufficiently flexible to express the tenth part of the many-sidedness of twentieth-century life.

W. Eilir Evans, 'Newspapers and Magazines in Wales', in
Wales Today and Tomorrow, ed. T. Stephens, 1907

399   All Celtic peoples are, at heart, Communists.

Keir Hardie, 'Socialism and the Celt'

400   Socialism means that the land of Wales will again belong to its people.

401   It is only too true that, as soon as English gets a footing in the Welsh home, it sets about, like the cuckoo fledgeling, to oust the old language from its own nest.

H. M. Hughes, 'The Bilingual Difficulty'

402   Wales must be barbarized!

Augustus John, 'Art in Wales'

403   And yet I sing my country,
        for Wales shall one day be
    the happiest and loveliest land,
        a time when we shall see
    no violent hand to waste her,
        no coward to betray her,
    no quarrelling to weaken her,
        and when Wales shall be free.*

John Morris-Jones, 'Cymru Fydd', 1907

404   The Welshwoman who has mastered the mysteries of the broth, and is acquainted with the various ways in which oatmeal

may be made palatable and digestible, may be said to have, for her purposes, finished her education in cookery.

> D. J. Nicholas, 'Welsh Home-Life', in *Wales Today and Tomorrow*, ed. T. Stephens, 1907

405   There is not a parish in Wales without its poet; scarcely a village of half a thousand inhabitants without its chaired bard.

406   The future of Wales is in the ink-bottle.*

> Richard Jones (Glaslyn), in *Cymru*, January 1907

407   While coal remains the most effective and economical source of power, and the population of the world increases, the position of Wales is assured.

> W. J. Perkins, 'Coal Trade and Shipping', in *Wales Today and Tomorrow*, ed.T. Stephens, 1907

408   Cardiff is a much abused and misrepresented city.

> J. Tertius Phillips, 'Drunkenness in Cardiff'

409   In the fruits of the Eisteddfod we have the most striking refutation of the argument that the use of Welsh keeps the Welsh people ignorant and narrow-minded.

> J. S. Popham, 'Should English People Learn Welsh?'

410   I am prepared to admit that the Eisteddfod has been of little use; and furthermore, from the bottom of my heart, do I hope that she never will be.

> J. Machreth Rees, 'The Eisteddfod'

411   May God make Wales a victorious people through the victory of the death of Christ. Let us continue praying that the Arm of the Lord be revealed, and that a holy shout of victory shall echo and re-echo throughout the valleys of Wales.

> Evan Roberts, 'What Wales Needs – Religiously'

412   When any great Imperial question arises, the Welsh recognize no interests apart from those of the whole of the United Kingdom.

> Thomas Stephens, in introduction

413   Unless some movement can be made in this direction, or employing artists of Wales upon Welsh work and Welsh themes, Welsh painting and sculpture can only become what Welsh music

has become, an echo – a fainter reflex, of the art of our pre-
dominant neighbour.

T. H. Thomas, 'Art in Wales'

414   Wales is as conservative in theology as it is liberal in party-
politics.

Iona Williams, 'Authority and Liberal Theology'

415   We know that some of the greatest heresies have been Welsh.

T. Charles Williams, 'The Influence of the Higher Criticism
upon Welsh Preaching'

416   The Welsh prefer philosophy to philology; music and poetry
to both.

417   The Church [of England] . . . which today, unrepentant at
heart and unchanged in action, sets its face against any national
movement and every national aspiration, is not, and cannot be, in
any true and real sense, the Church of the Welsh people.

W. Llewelyn Williams, 'The Church in Wales'

418   The Protestant Nonconformity of the Welsh people, as lived
and taught by their religious teachers during the last two centuries
. . . has preserved them from ignorance, lawlessness and irreligion,
and made of them one of the most scripturally enlightened, loyal
and religious nations on the surface of the earth.

David Davies, *Echoes from the Welsh Hills*, 1908

419   Wales has drawn more inspiration into its song from defeat
than from victory.*

Ben Bowen, 'Duw yn Ateb', *Rhyddiaith Ben Bowen*,
ed. David Bowen, 1909

420   God punishes those who neglect the language of their country;
because of that the Welsh of Radnorshire and Breconshire and the
borders are so much lower in understanding, in morals and in
religion than the Welsh of the most Welsh part of the principality.*

Robert Ambrose Jones (Emrys ap Iwan), *Homiliau*, 1909

421   An ancient folk, speaking an ancient speech,
     And cherishing in their bosoms all their past,
     Yet in whose fiery love of their own land
     No hatred of another finds a place.

Sir William Watson, 'Wales: a Greeting', 1909

422 Mr Keir Hardie's election colours are Red, White and Green. Red represents Labour in revolt. Green represents Nature and Nationalism, Home Rule for Ireland and for Wales. White represents Strength and Purity.

bulletin at General Election, January 1910

423 No people were ever less fitter to call a country their own and themselves a nation than the Welsh.

Arthur Tyssilio Johnson, *The Perfidious Welshman*, 1910

424 Few people can tell a lie to your face with such perfect composure as a Welshman.

425 It is as a poacher of fish that a Welshman excels.

426 The Welsh police-court is known all over the world as a very hotbed of perjury.

427 Like vultures coming out of the distant blue to congregate around the carcase of the tottering horse or stricken bullock which they have marked for their own, these Welsh men and women flock to the scene of the funeral to fill their insatiable gullets with the carrion of morbid curiosity.

428 Wales has had no great women of good repute.

429 If it should ever be your misfortune to have to spend Sunday in Wales, always get to windward when the chapels are disgorging the faithful.

430 Keep Taffy at arm's length, or he will take liberties, and become familiar; not only that, remember, he spits copiously and dangerously when moved by any slight emotion.

431 It is mainly the bigotry and the revolting ignorance of the dissenting parson which are responsible for the perpetuation of the hoggish manners common to the natives of Wales.

432 The Welsh, though they may sing their mournful hymns in a minor key at street corners, are not in any high sense musicians.

433 The world has never produced a more unscrupulous and self-interested hypocrite than the Welsh Member of Parliament

who springs from Nonconformist stock. He has all the wiles of a serpent and the slipperiness of an eel.

434   The visitor to Wales may go into a hundred cottages and find no books except a Bible, some commentaries, and perhaps a volume of sermons by a local preacher.

435   To any one who does not know the shallow transparency of the average Welsh mind, its utter want of ballast and lack of independence, the humbug with which the Welsh Member of Parliament feeds his herd of ignorant voters is almost beyond comprehension.

436   The political power of landlordism in Wales was shattered as effectively as the power of the Druids.
David Lloyd George, of the General Election of 1868,
in a speech, 1910

437   No Welsh boy can well read the history of his ancestors – so stirring a record of so stubborn a race, such a good, grim, fighting race – without feeling that it is good to be a Cymro.
Robert Scourfield Mills (Owen Rhoscomyl), *Flame-Bearers of Welsh History*, 1910

438   Cymru, then, is the right name for our country, meaning the Land of the Cymro . . . Cymro, then, is the right name, and the proud name, for every honourable man of us today.

439   There is no part of the British Empire where there is a greater diffusion of democratic sentiment than in the Principality of Wales, nor is there a portion of the King's realms where loyalty to the throne is deeper and more fervid . . . The badge of conquest which the first investiture [of 1284] wrought has, under the magic touch of King George, apotheosised into a jewel of royal favour, to be prized as a priceless legacy by future generations of Welshmen.
J. Hugh Edwards, *Wales*, 1911

440   Wales is to have an Investiture as a reminder that an English King and his robber barons strove for ages to destroy the Welsh people, and finally succeeded in robbing them of their lands, driving them into the mountain fastnesses of their native land like hunted beasts . . . The ceremony ought to make every Welshman who is patriotic blush with shame.
Keir Hardie, in speech at Tonypandy, 1 May 1911

441 Men and women of Dowlais: the National Party I have in mind is this: the people of Wales fighting to recover possession of the land of Wales; the working classes acquiring possession of the mines, the furnaces, and the railways, of the great public works generally, and working there as comrades, not for the benefit of shareholders, but for the good of every man, woman and child within your borders. That is the kind of nationalism that I want to see brought about. And when that comes, the Red Dragon will be emblazoned on the Red Flag of Socialism, the International Emblem of the working-class movement of the world.

Keir Hardie, in speech at Dowlais, Merthyr Tydfil, 14 October 1911

442 The traveller in Wales cannot fail to be struck with two things – namely, the romantic beauty of the country and the absolute lack of romance exhibited by the people.

T. W. H. Crosland, *Taffy was a Welshman*, 1912

443 According to all accounts, it was Offa who built a dyke to separate Wales from England, and we are inclined to think that Offa was a man of sense and discernment.

444 The fact is that Wales is a little land, and the Welsh are a little people, with little intellects and little views.

445 Considered as a spectacle pure and simple, an Eisteddfod is a pitiful and almost squalid affair.

446 The difference between England and Wales is that England consists of an upper class, a middle class and a democracy, while Wales is a democracy pure and simple.

447 The Welsh resemble the modern Greeks in this respect, that they appear to devour newspapers with the appetite of the cormorant.

448 When it pleases him – and it quite frequently does please him – Mr Lloyd George can be very proud of his Welshness.

449 It is time we remembered that England is our messuage and demesne, and not the backyard of Mr Ellis Griffiths, and that Englishmen were born to rule and not to be ruled, and least of all to be ruled by a bumptious, snuffling, flighty, tiresome, fifth-rate bunch of barbarians like the Welsh.

450   If Welsh is killed, it will be killed in the house of its friends.*
Robert Ambrose Jones (Emrys ap Iwan), quoted by
T. Gwynn Jones in *Emrys ap Iwan: Cofiant*, 1912

451   Wales is a land of poets, but it's the poets who say that.*
T. E. Nicholas, 'Beirdd Cymru', in *Y Geninen*,
vol. 31, no. 3, July 1913

452   Stick it, the Welsh!
battle-cry in First World War, 1914–18

453   The South Wales miner is a very real factor in the Nation's
fighting strength and his loyalty in this crisis is well nigh
indispensable to the State.
editorial in *The Times*, 24 August 1914

454   The greatest service Wales can render to the world is to be
herself to the last drop of her blood.
Granville Barker, in *Cambrian Daily Leader*, 13 June 1914

455   The next Shakespeare and Goethe may be born in Wales.
George Bernard Shaw, 'On Welsh Drama', in
South Wales Daily News, 13 June 1914

456   Everything that is narrow and ignorant and ridiculous and
dishonest in Wales will be castigated ruthlessly in the Welsh
national theatre, and the process will not be popular with the
narrow, the ignorant, the bigoted and the ridiculous.

457   Lloyd George knew my father, Father knew Lloyd George.
popular song, sung to the tune of
'Onward, Christian soldiers', *c*.1915

458   Wales would be brighter and more Christianlike if every
chapel were burnt to the ground and a public-house raised on the
ashes thereof.
Caradoc Evans, in letter to *Western Mail*,
27 November 1915

459   The peculiar Welsh temperament, essentially imaginative,
intellectual and impatient, manifests itself continually in industrial
disputes.
Stanley Jevons, *The British Coal Trade*, 1915

460   The revival of the Welsh national spirit will lead to a closer union with England.

K. V. Jones, Life of John Viriamu Jones, 1915

461   I am only a bit of a Welshman in an office in London.*

David Lloyd George, in speech at National Eisteddfod,
Bangor, 1915

462   The idea of nationality and of religion would seem in danger of being repudiated in some of the industrial districts in favour of an illusory idea of a cosmopolitan, and perhaps to some extent, materialistic brotherhood.

D. Lleufer Thomas, in speech at the National Eisteddfod, 1915

463   Make me content
       With some sweetness
       From Wales
       Whose nightingales
       Have no wings.

Edward Thomas, 'Words', 1915

464   Wales is such a particular part of England.*

Papal encyclical, 1916

465   The Welshman has many vices, and drinking is not one of them.

Caradoc Evans, 'The Welsh Miner', in
New Witness, 7 December 1916

466   The English language is associated in my mind with tyranny.

T. Gwynn Jones, in Welsh Outlook, April 1916

467   Now The Times is not exactly the organ of the Welsh peasantry.

David Lloyd George, in speech at the National Eisteddfod,
Aberystwyth, 17 August 1916

468   The Welshman's truth is more in the nature of a curve than a straight line.

Walter Hinds Page, in speech, c.1916

469   Helen of the roads,
       The mountain ways of Wales,
       And the Mabinogion tales
       Is one of the true gods.

Edward Thomas, 'Roads', 1916

470   To fight for the freedom of the Belgian, it is not absolutely necessary to oppress and bully the Welshman.

editorial in *Welsh Outlook*, February 1917

471   It is sometimes said that west of Newtown, the spirit of enterprise does not exist.

May 1917

472   Not one Welshman has produced fiction which has lived six months after the day of its publication.

Caradoc Evans, in a letter to *Western Mail*, 23 January 1917

473   I write because I believe that the cesspools of West Wales should be stirred up, because I want to see my people freed from religious tyranny, because I love my country so much that I would exhibit her sores that they may be healed.

474   Workers of the Vale of Amman,
       Echo Russia's mighty thrust:
    Strike a blow for Cambria's freedom,
       Bring oppression to the dust.

John Harris, 'Welsh Workers, Arise!', 1917

475   Forty years ago, the conviction that the Welsh language was doomed to die was prevalent among prominent Welshmen. No man who is at all competent to judge believes that today.

John M. Jones, in *Welsh Outlook*, February 1917

476   If Welsh nationalism allows the period after the war to pass without an effort to obtain autonomy . . . there will be a plausible argument for saying that the Welsh people themselves regard their nationalism merely as an amiable sentiment and not as a political matter.

477   Labour believes in self-government. The Labour Party is pledged to a scheme of statutory legislatures for Scotland, Wales and Ireland, as part of the larger plan which will transform the British Empire into a Commonwealth of self-governing nations.

manifesto of Labour Party at General Election, 1918

478   Given self-government, Wales might establish itself as a modern Utopia and develop its own institutions, its own culture,

its own ideal of democracy in politics, industry and social life, as an example and an inspiration to the rest of the world.

Arthur Henderson, in statement by Transport House, June 1918

479   One of the most important measures of reconstruction after the war should be national self-determination within this kingdom.

Ramsay MacDonald MP, in speech in the House of Commons, 1918

480   In days when Bohemia and Poland are being reconstituted as democratic republics, Wales cannot accept as a substitute for self-government a new Court of the Marches set up in the backroom of some dingy office in Whitehall.

editorial in *Welsh Outlook*, March 1919

481   It [the National Eisteddfod] encourages vulgarity of mind because it allows . . . the nation's leaders, from the Prime Minister down, to be self-complacent and self-congratulatory and smugly to tell us, year in year out, what a wonderful little people we really are.

August 1919

482   The voice of Welsh Nationalism and Tory democracy.

motto of *Western Mail* on the occasion of its
fiftieth anniversary, 1919

483   We were simply robbed of our birthright by a foreign system of education and its paid servants . . . Our system of education was moulded to help the few favoured ones to get on in the world.

J. Tywi Jones, in *Welsh Outlook*, December 1919

484   We [the British] have muddled along tolerably well for ten centuries . . . Why should the Scots and Welsh give up governing the Empire to send them back to the insignificant task of governing their own country?

F. E. Smith MP, in speech in the House of Commons,
April 1919

485   A considerable measure of Devolution on national lines can alone satisfy the national aspirations of Scotland and Wales.

three of the signatories of a report of the Speaker's Conference
on Devolution, 1920

486 Not on the battlefield but in literature a Llywelyn and a Glyndŵr are needed.*

Owen M. Edwards, 'Angen Mwyaf Cymru', in
Yn y Wlad ac Ysgrifau Eraill, 1921

487 The Welsh are a lively, energetic nation, full of imagination and skill; but, for all their enthusiasm, they are a timid nation when it comes to taking a step forward. They know they can show the way to other nations; but their old cowardly habit is to look for paths already trodden, and often to seek alien leaders to take them on their way.*

'Prifysgol y Gweithwyr'

488 The leaders of Irish nationalism live a great deal of their time in gaol and many of them die on the gallows. In Wales they live in comfort and die with a considerable amount of property to dispose of in their wills.

editorial in *Welsh Outlook*, January 1922

489 Wales is called upon to fit herself for the supreme task of being the moral and spiritual driving force among the nations of the world.

Gwilym Davies, in *Welsh Outlook*, January 1922

490 I shall be faithful to Wales, to my fellow man, and to Christ.*

Ifan ab Owen Edwards, motto of Urdd Gobaith Cymru,
founded in 1922

491 The spirit of Wales is born in the mountain farmhouse, in the cottage by the brook, in the coal-miner's home.*

Owen M. Edwards, *Er Mwyn Cymru*, 1922

492 Wales has her own language and, without it, she cannot keep her soul. For it is not merely a collection of words . . . Within it are treasured the poetry of life and the hope of a thousand years.*

493 Resolutions will never achieve Home Rule – resolution will.

Ernest Hughes, in *Welsh Outlook*, May 1922

494 Unless Wales comes into contact with the Continent, unless she knows what the great world beyond the borders of Wales and England is thinking, in vain will be our hope for a literary renaissance.*

Griffith John Williams, 'Cyfres y Werin', in
Y Llenor, vol. 1, no. 1, Spring 1922

495 The Eisteddfod and the Gorsedd have for years been the nursery of quackery, and no institution that nurtures quackery can flourish and bear fruit.*

'Yr Eisteddfod a'r Orsedd', in *Y Llenor*, vol. 1, no. 2, Summer 1922

496 We Welsh people are sadly prone to expend ourselves in vague benediction. In this Drama Movement, we need less oratory and more carpentry. The man with the 'hwyl' is now not so useful as the man with a hammer.

J. O. Francis, in Transactions of the Honourable Society of Cymmrodorion, 1923–4

497 It would be a great blessing for Wales if some Welshman did something for his nation that caused him to be put in prison.*

Saunders Lewis, in speech at meeting of Cymdeithas y Tair G in Mold, 1923

498 You hear better singing and more tuneful music in a third-class revue than at the National Eisteddfod . . . an ill-managed circus.

Caradoc Evans, 'A Tilt at the Eisteddfod', in *Western Mail*, 2 June 1924

499 In that Martyr's Town [Merthyr Tydfil] in Glamorgan everybody was a bitter politician by the time he had done teething. There were no neutrals among us above six months old.

J. O. Francis, 'The Glory of Glamorgan', in *The Legend of the Welsh*, 1924

500 Thus did Keir Hardie appear among us – bearing a new torch.

501 Our compatriots in North Wales, where the Iberian strain is now thinnest, view us South Welshmen with a dubious eye, for to them we appear a rather obstreperous community . . . To the Southerner there is in North Wales a restraint which he cannot quite understand and which, to him, seems to border on passivity. Which region has the greater final wisdom the oracles have not yet revealed.

'Mr Hergesheimer's Welshmen'

502 In all the thirteen counties there is still the lingering suspicion that the London Welshman is a prodigal who has left his father's home to go into a far country.

'Wales and the London Welsh'

503   In nine cases out of ten the Welshman who loses his Welsh will probably not exchange it for the language of Shakespeare at all. What he will get in exchange will be . . . the language of the *Daily Mail*; not the poetry of Milton or Shelley, but the faded inanities of the London music-halls; not the fine flower of cosmopolitan culture, but the brainless, heartless, hopeless vacuity of English suburbia.

H. Idris Bell, *Welsh Poems in English*, 1925

504   Cardiff is a devil of a place for plays. Actors come away from it subdued to silence.

St John Ervine, in *Western Mail*, 5 October 1925

505   I *hate* Wales, I tell you – and the Welsh. I hate them more than any other place and people because they are my own whom I have tried to love.

Rhys Lloyd,
in Hilda Vaughan, *The Battle to the Weak*, 1925

506   Welsh will live or die, not in the schools, but on the hearths of the people.

editorial in *Welsh Outlook*, January 1926

507   We have had no architecture, hardly any painting, and very little music until quite recently; the culture of Wales has always been a literary culture, and it depends on the Welsh language and the use that is made of it.*

W. J. Gruffydd, in editorial in *Y Llenor*, vol. 5, no. 2, Summer 1926

508   The University of Wales is further from the thought and culture of its own nation than any other university in the world.*

509   What then is our nationalism? . . . To fight not for Welsh independence but for the civilization of Wales. To claim for Wales not independence but freedom.*

Saunders Lewis, *Egwyddorion Cenedlaetholdeb*, 1926

510   And as for Anglo-Welsh literature, I blush for my country at seeing any of it in print.*

W. J. Gruffydd, in editorial in *Y Llenor*, vol. 6, no. 1, Spring 1927

511   I would not mind if dock-leaves or dandelions were the emblems of my country. I do not need, thanks to my upbringing, to wear anything to show that I am a Welshman.*

W. J. Gruffydd, in editorial in *Y Llenor*, vol. 6, no. 2, Summer 1927

512   I am quite convinced that as a nation we suffer badly from the inferiority complex of the peasant, and that it is a fairly recent thing in our history.*

W. J. Gruffydd, in editorial in *Y Llenor*, vol. 6, no. 4, Winter 1927

513   Any fool can be a crown bard of Wales, because genius is low in Wales.

David Emrys James (Dewi Emrys), reported in
The Sunday Express, 25 April 1927

514   The coal valleys [of south Wales] bear the marks, psychological as well as physical, of having been the arena for a scramble by everybody, high and low, for quick money.

Anonymous contributor to *The Times*, 2 April 1927

515   Wales finds it difficult to learn the simple lesson that no one will take her seriously until we learn a little of the dignity of silence.*

W. J. Gruffydd, in editorial in *Y Llenor*, vol. 7, no. 4,
Winter 1928

516   No one can be expected to buy and read Welsh books for patriotic reasons alone.*

Kate Roberts, 'Y Nofel Gymraeg', in *Y Llenor*, vol. 7, no. 4,
Winter 1928

517   From earliest times the Welsh have been looked upon as an unclean people. It is thus they have preserved their racial integrity.

Dr Fagan,
in Evelyn Waugh, *Decline and Fall*, 1928

518   The Welsh are the only nation in the world that has produced no graphic or plastic art, no architecture, no drama. They just sing . . . sing and blow down wind instruments of plated silver.

519   These Welshmen are peculiar. They won't stand being shouted at, They'll do anything if you explain the reason for it – do and die, but they have to know the reason why. The best way to make them behave is not to give them too much time to think. Work them off their feet.

Captain Dunn,
in Robert Graves, *Goodbye to All That*, 1929

520   They began singing. Instead of the usual music-hall songs

they sang Welsh hymns, each man taking a part. The Welsh always sang when pretending not to be scared; it kept them steady. And they never sang out of tune.

521   Modern Wales has taken its standards from the only English class which would readily give it conversation and friendship, and that was the English Nonconformists of the industrial towns. The ideal we have thus accepted is the quintessence of bourgeois mediocrity.

Saunders Lewis, in *Welsh Outlook*, October 1929

522   Give [Wales] self-government and you will give her a capital where her writers will congregate and meet artists and form a society. Give her a government and a capital and she will in time gather an urban class which will be the basis of a new Welsh aristocracy.

523   Welshmen in their chapels do not kneel in prayer. They bend down, sitting as though they are vomiting.

524   Welsh Nationalism should be able to include people of conservative mind as well as people of progressive mind, like the nationalism of every other country.*

W. J. Gruffydd, in editorial in *Y Llenor*, vol. 9, no. 1,
Spring 1930

525   Where there is civilization, there is Welsh coal.

editorial in *Welsh Outlook*, April 1931

526   It is easy to love Wales when you are far away from it making a fortune in England.*

W. J. Gruffydd, in editorial in *Y Llenor*, vol. 10, no. 1,
Spring 1931

527   If a nation that has lost its political machinery becomes content to express its nationality henceforward only in the sphere of literature and the arts, then that literature and those arts will very quickly become provincial and unimportant, mere echoes of the ideas and artistic movements of the neighbouring and dominant nation. This danger is very real for Wales today.

Saunders Lewis, *The Banned Wireless Talk on Welsh
Nationalism*, 1931

528   I do not think the Welsh language will disappear rapidly,

even if that should happen. But it will cease to be a language worth cultivating. Its literature will become entirely second-hand and fifth-rate. Believe me, there is something worse and more tedious than the death of a language, and that is its functionless survival.

529   What the Welsh today and tomorrow need is a call to heroism. The heroic note has not been heard in Welsh politics. But it is the only note that can save us now.

530   Welsh Nationalism has become the spare-time hobby of corpulent and successful men.
Saunders Lewis, in editorial in *The Welsh Nationalist*, January 1932

531   How can I convey to the reader, who does not know him [David Lloyd George], any just impression of this extraordinary figure of our time, this syren, this goat-footed bard, this half-human visitor to our age from the hag-ridden magic and enchanted woods of Celtic antiquity?
J. M. Keynes, *Essays and Sketches in Biography*, 1933

532   The certain effect of killing the Welsh language will be the enhancement of the victory of capitalism.*
Saunders Lewis, in *Y Ddraig Goch*, August 1933

533   We want to free Wales from the grip of the English. We want to de-Anglicize Wales.*
'Un Iaith i Gymru'

534   That English is a spoken language in Wales is an evil, an unmixed evil. It must be wiped out from the land of Wales; delenda est Carthago.*

535   Agriculture should be the principal industry of Wales and the basis of its civilization.*
'Deg Pwynt Polisi'

536   For the sake of the moral health of Wales and the moral and physical well-being of its population, south Wales must be de-industrialized.*

537   Shortly after the extinction of the monoglot Welsh, the life of the Welsh language will come to an end.*

538   It's impossible for me to tell you how much I want to get out

of it all, out of the narrowness and dirtiness, out of the eternal ugliness of the Welsh people and all that belongs to them, out of the pettiness of a mother I don't care for and the giggling batch of relatives . . . I shall have to get out soon or there will be no need. I'm sick and this bloody country's killing me.

Dylan Thomas, in letter to Pamela Hansford Johnson,
October 1933

539 First and foremost, speak in platitudes.*

W. J. Gruffydd, advice to speakers at St David's Day dinners,
in editorial in *Y Llenor*, vol. 13, no. 1, Spring 1934

540 Wales was Christian and Catholic even before she was Welsh . . . and I see the mark of her Catholic formation upon the whole of her history and culture.*

Saunders Lewis, *Catholigiaeth a Chymru*, 1934

541 Thus . . . it always was with literature in Wales . . . when something new arrives, it is stamped upon at first, and then imitated to death.*

T. Gwynn Jones, 'Cymru a'r Drama', *Beirniadaeth a
Myfyrdod*, 1935

542 South Wales should be scheduled as a Grand National Ruin.

Thomas Jones CH, in *New Statesman and Nation*, 1935

543 The tendency of the Welsh-speaking Welsh is to refuse to face the artistic problems of our industrial areas and to try to escape from them by considering them as un-Welsh phenomena.*

Alun Llywelyn-Williams, in editorial in *Tir Newydd*, no. 3,
Autumn 1935

544 He scorned his land, his tongue denied;
        Nor Welsh nor English, lived and died
A bastard mule, and made his own
        Each mulish fault save this alone:
Dic somehow got, that prince of fools,
        A vast vile progeny of mules.*

Thomas Jacob Thomas (Sarnicol), 'Dic Siôn Dafydd', 1935

545 . . . this race of quarrelsome nightingales.

H. A. L. Fisher, of the Welsh, *History of Europe*, 1936

546   The Welsh are still an old-fashioned, conservative people, who have never been exploited, in literature at least.
Edward Garnett, in letter to Geraint Goodwin, 24 March 1936

547   Wales is such a small country and we all know one another so well that it becomes more and more difficult as a man grows older, and widens the circle of his acquaintance, to offer a fairly honest opinion on topics of the day.*
W. J. Gruffydd, in editorial in *Y Llenor*, vol. 15, no. 1, Spring 1936

548   How sad it is that a Welshman should be an exile in Wales, for every Welshman living in Cardiff or its suburbs is an exile.*
W. J. Gruffydd, *Hen Atgofion*, 1936

549   The English Government's behaviour in the matter of the Llŷn bombing range is exactly the behaviour of this new Anti-Christ throughout Europe. And in this assize-court in Caernarfon today we, the accused in this dock, are challenging Anti-Christ. We deny the absolute power of the State-God. Here in Wales, a land that has no tradition except Christian tradition, a land that has never in all its history been pagan or atheist, we stand for the preservation of that Christian tradition and for the supremacy of the moral law over the power of materialist bureaucracy. So that whether you find us guilty or not guilty is of importance today for the future of Christian civilization and Christian liberty and Christian justice in Europe.*
Saunders Lewis, in speech from the dock, Caernarfon,
13 October 1936

550   This was the weakness of his own people: they had a heroic capacity for suffering, but it did not extend to acting against the cause of that suffering.*
Kate Roberts, *Traed mewn Cyffion*, 1936

551   Wales is a beautiful mother, but she can be a dangerously possessive wife.
Rhys Davies, *My Wales*, 1937

552   It is well known that Welsh people are vigorously unable to tolerate any criticism of their land from their native writers.

553   The Welsh are the finest full-time actors in the world. But we have no theatre. We do not need one; life is a large enough stage for us.

554   There is still a primitive shine on Wales; one can smell the old world there still, and it is not a dead aroma.

555   There is something sadistic about a Sunday in Aberystwyth.

556   To me it is a lovely tongue [Welsh] to be cultivated in the same way as some people cultivate orchids, or keep Persian cats: a hobby yielding much private delight and sometimes a prize in an exhibition.

557   The writing of Welsh is entirely a part-time job, a hobby, undertaken mostly by university professors and ministers of the Gospel.

558   There is no decadence in Wales, save that imposed upon it by the diseases of modern industrialization.

559   Garmon, Garmon,
    A vineyard placed in my care is Wales, my country,
    To deliver unto my children
    And my children's children
    Intact, an eternal heritage;
    And behold, the swine rush on her to rend her.
    Now I will call on my friends,
    Scholars and simple folk,
    'Take your place by my side in the breach
    That the age-old splendour be kept for ages to come.'
    And this, my Lord, is the vineyard of our beloved, too;
    From Llan Fair to Llan Fair, a land where the Faith
                       is established.*
              Saunders Lewis, *Buchedd Garmon*, 1937

560   If you are content with the creation of an Anglo-Welsh literature of value, giving expression to Welsh feelings and experiences, but through the medium of English, then you will have provided an excellent excuse for those who would acquiesce in the death of the Welsh language . . . In the end one might even see 'Welsh' studies in the University Colleges of Wales represented by a lecturer in Anglo-Welsh Literature in the English Department.*
        Seosamh Mac Grianna, *An Breatain Bheag*, 1937

561   Though we write in English, we are rooted in Wales.
        Keidrych Rhys, in editorial in *Wales*, no. 1, Summer 1937

562   I stood in the ruins of Dowlais
     And sighed for the lovers destroyed
     And the landscape of Gwalia stained for all time
     By the bloody hand of progress.

> Idris Davies, *Gwalia Deserta*, 1938

563   From the south [of Wales] comes every revolution, in religion and literature, but it is in the north that the revolution is fully developed.*

> W. J. Gruffydd, *Owen Morgan Edwards: Cofiant*, 1938

564   Why have you given us this misery,
     The pain like leaden weights on flesh and blood?
     Your language on our shoulders like a sack,
     And your tradition shackles round our feet?*

> D. Gwenallt Jones, 'Cymru' (trans. Joseph P. Clancy), 1938

565   We are a long way from the world in Wales, and there is a kind of apathy about things. The poor accept their lot and the well-to-do their comfort. And the farmers pray only for rain. I would like to wake them up.

> Alun Lewis, in a letter to Jean Gilbert, 12 May 1938

566   We deny the right of England to push Wales into war once again. Nobody is threatening Wales, and over the centuries Wales has seen only the worst of England.*

> editorial in *Heddiw*, June 1939

567   To say that Wales is a nation and not a state is to emphasize that it remains a soul without a body.

> Gwilym Davies, 'Beyond our Frontiers', in *The Welsh Review*,
> vol. 1, no. 2, March 1939

568   The Land of Mountains is a place for old people, and for young people who have come home to die of tuberculosis.*

> W. J. Gruffydd, in editorial in *Y Llenor*, vol. 18, no. 1, Spring 1939

569   We are now a bilingual nation, and thus we rely upon English for literature of courage and magnanimity, and keep the Welsh language to express things that are harmless and wishy-washy, poetry and prose which can be expected some day to be the set books of the Central Welsh Board.*

> W. J. Gruffydd, in editorial in *Y Llenor*, vol. 18, no. 3,
> Autumn 1939

570   It is better, even for the language, to have a right-thinking Englishman than a wrong-headed Welshman.*

571   Welsh ought to be the first language of all of us Welshmen – but it isn't, and most are afraid that it never will be.
> Gwyn Jones, in editorial in *The Welsh Review*, vol. 1, no. 1,
> February 1939

572   The Englishman is bad at learning languages, the Welshman good; the Englishman in these affairs is thick-skinned, the Welshman courteous; in a free mingling of the two peoples the English language must triumph.
> Gwyn Jones, in editorial in *The Welsh Review*, vol. 2, no. 4,
> November 1939

573   From Merthyr to Dowlais the tramway climbs,
> A slug's slime-trail over the slag-heaps.
> What's nowadays a desert of cinemas,
> Rain over disused tips, this once was Wales.*
>> Saunders Lewis, 'Y Dilyw, 1939' (trans. Anthony Conran), 1939

574   Knowing neither language nor dialect, feeling no insult,
> We gave our masterpiece to history in our country's MPs.*

575   There is abundant intellectual ability in Wales, but there is a catastrophic lack of moral courage and decision.
> Saunders Lewis, *Is There an Anglo-Welsh Literature?*, 1939

576   Mr Dylan Thomas is obviously an equipped writer, but there is nothing hyphenated about him. He belongs to the English.

577   Whatever culture there has been in the mining valleys of South Wales has been the remnant of the social life of the country-side, and has been Welsh in speech. The extension of English has everywhere accompanied the decay of that culture, the loss of social traditions and of social unity and the debasement of spiritual values. It has produced no richness of idiom, no folk-song, but has battened on the spread of journalese and the mechanised slang of the talkies.

578   Owain Glyndŵr said all there is to be said for this country hundreds of years ago. Wales for the Wales. More of him and less of Mr Marx, please.
> Gwilym Morgan,
> in Richard Llewellyn, *How Green Was My Valley*, 1939

579   How green was my Valley, then, and the Valley of them that
have gone.

580   The point which it behoves all Anglo-Welsh writers to
remember is that there would be no Anglo-Welsh literature at all if
the Welsh language hadn't been a living language for so long.

John Cowper Powys, 'Welsh Culture', in *The Welsh Review*,
vol. 1, no. 5, June 1939

581   For generations the heart of the Englishman towards the
Welshman has been one of open distrust, and the heart of the
Welshman towards the Englishman one of civility and covert
contempt.

Llewelyn Powys, 'Welsh and English', in *The Welsh Review*,
vol. 1, no. 3, April 1939

582   The Welsh are a nation of toughs, rogues, and poetic
humbugs, vivid in their speech, impulsive in behaviour, riddled
with a sly and belligerent tribalism.

V. S. Pritchett, in *The New Statesman and Nation*, 1939

583   The Welsh nation was born in and of the Roman Empire.
Rome is our mother.

A. W. Wade-Evans, 'What the Welsh Nation has Forgotten', in
The Welsh Review, vol. 1, no. 1, February 1939

584   The Welsh nation has suffered much at the hands of
historians.

585   The literary life of Wales suffers from what Pharaoh would
call minor plagues.

J. Ellis Williams, 'Welsh Drama Today', in *The Welsh Review*,
vol. 2, no. 1, August 1939

586   If Wales were half as enthusiastic in the work of putting its
own life in order as it is in serving at the tables of foreigners, Wales
would be much more like what we have in mind when talking
about a Christian country.*

editorial in *Heddiw*, September–October 1940

587   Nonconformity and Liberalism are not a religion; they are a
wrangle designed to keep us in subjection.

Caradoc Evans, entry in journal, *c*.1940

588   There has never been a great Welsh criminal.

589   Wales England wed, so I was bred.
                         Ernest Rhys, epigraph to *Wales England Wed*, 1940

590   The Welsh people of today are still emerging from the nineteenth century.
                         Llewelyn Wyn Griffith, *Word from Wales*, 1941

591   The Welsh novel is in a poor way, and Wales is still waiting for its great novelist.

592   We are merely asking England to be a good neighbour and to allow us to cultivate our garden in our own fashion.

593   There is no Society for the Abolition of Welsh: there is no enemy but indifference, the inertia of all administration, the unwillingness to provide for bilingualism. It is so much less trouble to pretend that the other language does not exist.

594   If the [German] victors saw fit to give us some semblance of independence, as Brittany has been promised, it would not be out of love for Wales but in order to weaken England. And then we would be under the feet of our own Quislings in Wales, with neither parliament nor Whitehall to raise a finger in favour of the common people. I cannot think of a blacker prospect.*
                         W. J. Gruffydd, in editorial in *Y Llenor*, vol. 20, no. 1, Spring 1941

595   The quarry villages like Llanllechid and Bethesda are no different from the mining villages in the South.
                         Alun Lewis, in letter to Brenda Chamberlain, 21 February 1941

596   St Michael, who loves the hills, pray for Wales,
       St Michael, friend of the sick, remember us.*
                         Saunders Lewis, 'Haf Bach Mihangel'
                         (trans. Joseph P. Clancy), 1941

597   It is hereby enacted that the Welsh language may be used in any court in Wales by any party or witness who considers that he would otherwise be at any disadvantage by reason of his natural language of communication being Welsh.
                         Welsh Courts Act, 1942

598   We are not living in normal times, but the Welshman has not

lived a normal life for more than four centuries.*
editorial in Heddiw, December 1941–January 1942

599   Lightning
Is different in Wales.
Keidrych Rhys, 'Youth', 1942

600   I know no love for disembodied principles, improbable tales,
The strength of the common man was always the strength of
Wales.
Keidrych Rhys, 'Tragic Guilt', 1942

601   I prefer to be a little backward on that matter.
Winston Churchill, on appointing a Secretary of State for
Wales, in speech in the House of Commons, 1943

602   Who loves not the land of his birth
Should hide himself in the earth.
Who loves not these derelict vales
Is no true son of eternal Wales.
Idris Davies, The Angry Summer, 1943

603   A man is greater than his country. Therefore, I do not exist
for Wales, but Wales exists for me.
Rhys Davies, 'From my Notebook', in Wales, no. 2, October 1943

604   Amateurs are the curse of art in Wales.

605   There is only one abiding classic: Wales.

606   For every minute the present Parliament gives Wales, the
Welsh Parliament would give a month.
Gwynfor Evans, 'Rebuild from the Foundations',
in Wales, no. 2, October 1943

607   Wales shares with Estonia the inestimable advantage of
being small enough to be properly governed.

608   The decentralisation from Whitehall should be canalised
into the creation of a Welsh Office, with a Secretary of State of
Cabinet rank. It is along these lines that real hope lies for the
largest measure of effective self-government in Wales.
James Griffiths MP, 'Wales after the War', in Wales, no. 1, July 1943

609   Over a great part of Wales, but not everywhere, there are places which have ceased to be Welsh and have not become English.

Llewelyn Wyn Griffith, 'A Note on "Anglo-Welsh"', in Wales,
no. 1, July 1943

610   The path of the Anglo-Welsh writer is a hard one, poor dab.

Glyn Jones, in review of Idris Davies, The Angry Summer, in
Wales, no. 1, July 1943

611   For Wales the permanent medium of literature should always be Welsh. Our separate identity ceases for us when the language ceases. Then what is the purpose of Anglo-Welsh literature? One purpose is this: it is not that we want to show the English in a small country way that we can beat them at their own language (that attitude is responsible largely for the growing gulf between the Welsh and Anglo-Welsh); but that we want to make them aware of Welsh differences and ventures, and that English is the only medium in which this can be done. A zealous group of Anglo-Welsh writers, properly co-ordinated, should be vaulable agents in securing sympathy in the better English minds for Welsh cultural ideals and aims. For we are going to need sympathy, even if we haven't any today.

Keidrych Rhys, in editorial in Wales, no. 2, October 1943

612   This sea town was my world; outside, a strange Wales, coal-pitted, mountained, river-run, full, so far as I knew, of choirs and football teams and sheep and story-book tall black hats and red flannel petticoats, moved about its business which was none of mine.

Dylan Thomas, 'Reminiscences of Childhood', broadcast
15 February 1943, Quite Early One Morning, 1954

613   When I talk about England, I always include the suburbs, Wales and Scotland.

E. C. Cobb MP, in speech in the House of Commons,
20 July 1944

614   I want self-government for Wales, but I want it for rather different reasons from the Welsh Nationalist Party . . . I want to see my Nation ridding itself of the cant and hypocrisy associated with its religious life, and I want to see at least seventy-five per cent of the places of worship in Wales pulled down or used in a more effective way.

Huw T. Edwards, 'What I Want for Wales', in Wales, no. 3, January 1944

615 I want to see at least twenty-five per cent of the people of the Rhondda Valleys compulsorily removed to new localities.

616 The only thing of real importance to Wales is – is she of real importance to herself?*

D. J. Williams, 'Y Ddau Genedlaetholdeb yng Nghymru', in
Y Llenor, vol. 23, nos. 3 and 4, Autumn/Winter 1944

617 Certainly, let us have a free Wales, but let it be populated by free Welsh. Let us have Wales for the Welsh, but not for Welsh politicians, Welsh owners, or the Welsh old men who still govern mental life through the chapels, the schools, and the universities.

George Woodcock, in letter to the editor, in *Wales*, no. 5,
Autumn 1944

618 Wales is a small nation which, through increasing difficulties, has preserved her language and cultural life through the centuries. The true freedom of Wales depends not only on political control of her own life, but on economic control as well. True freedom for Wales would be the result and product of a Socialist Britain and only under such conditions could self-government in Wales be an effective and secure guardian of the life of the nation.

manifesto of the Labour Party at General Election, 1945

619 As a man of action, resource, and creative energy, he [David Lloyd George] stood, when at his zenith, without a rival. His name is a household word throughout our Commonwealth of nations. He was the greatest Welshman which that unconquerable race has produced since the age of the Tudors. Much of his work abides, some of it will grow greatly in the future, and those who come after us will find the pillars of his life's toil upstanding, massive and indestructible.

Winston Churchill, in speech in the House of Commons, 1945

620 For all his sincerity and singleness of purpose, his personality forbids that he [Saunders Lewis] shall ever be a leader of the people. His intellectual pride, his icy contempt for those who do not walk beside, or behind, him, his lack of the common touch, and the authoritarian taint in politics and religion now associated with his name, these have set him aside from modern, democratic Wales. The personal tragedy of the man is that while earnestly desiring to unite Welshmen, he succeeds only in exacerbating and sundering them. He would give his life for Wales, but cannot give

Welshmen his charity: he has become the single greatest obstacle to his party's chance of becoming a party of the Welsh people. Yet history will find him his place, as a pioneer spirit and a patriot who never flinched from private hurt or public odium. Rejected by his people as their political leader, he may be after all the apostle of their new awakening.

Anonymous, in *The Welsh Review*, vol. 5, no. 4, Winter 1946

621   There has been too great a tendency to identify Welsh culture with Welsh speaking . . . What some of us are afraid of is that, if this psychosis is developed too far, we shall see in some of the English-speaking parts of Wales a vast majority tyrannised over by a few Welsh-speaking people in Cardiganshire . . . The whole of the Civil Service of Wales would be eventually provided from those small pockets of Welsh-speaking, Welsh-writing zealots and the vast majority of Welshmen would be denied participation in the government of their own country.

Aneurin Bevan, in speech in the House of Commons,
28 October 1946

622   If the working-man is the salt of the earth, the Welsh working-man is that salt ground to a sharp, astringent powder. He is born to a tradition of the hardest of grim punishing labour. He has the fortune, too, to be born to a kind of tradition of the spirit. Even at his lowest economic ebb, he has that thing which takes him through to much of his choir-practice and debating clubs, that gives him the impetus to read.

James Cameron, in *Daily Express*, 14 November 1946

623   We are by now well used to hearing the word 'national' coming from the lips of men who have never been over-energetic on behalf of Welsh nationalism in any other way.*

W. J. Gruffydd, in editorial in *Y Llenor*, vol. 25, nos. 1 and 2,
Spring–Summer 1946

624   Some professors have forgotten that the University was created to serve Wales, not Wales to serve the University, and many of our University authorities have seemed to be unduly anxious to turn Welshmen into Englishmen.

Griffith Hartwell Jones, *A Celt Looks at the World*, 1946

625   To our nostrils Conservative and Labour complacency about Wales have much the same smell.

Gwyn Jones, in editorial in *The Welsh Review*, vol. 5, no. 4, Winter 1946

626   We have today a large measure of self-government in our own hands. Why are we not better governed? Mainly because we are indifferent or incompetent, not because we are under the heel of England. That is the fact, and because it is unpleasant we don't want to look at it. We want to dodge it, we want to find a scapegoat.

Thomas Jones CH, *The Native Never Returns*, 1946

627   It is no good trying to preserve the language and the Welsh tradition by a political device like Dominion status. It will certainly antagonise as many as it conciliates. The past cannot be effaced and Wales will never be able to return to the narrow enclosed life it led of old. We shall not see in the lifetime of anyone now living the Welsh language as widely spoken in Monmouth-shire and Glamorgan as it is today in Cardiganshire.

628   We have to face the possibility not, I think, of the disappear-ance of Welsh, but of its inadequacy as a medium for expressing the complex phantasmagoria of modern life.

R. S. Thomas, 'Some Contemporary Scottish Writing', in
Wales, vol. 6, no. 3, 1946

629   It is true that the Welsh have a good reputation as a democratic people, but in my opinion they show all the weaknesses that belong to democracy.*

R. S. Thomas, 'Arian a Swydd', in *Y Fflam*, vol. 1, no. 1, 1946

630   To the artist, then, a sense of Welsh Nationhood should be consistent with a very definite attitude to life and affairs, namely the constant realization that he belongs to a country of great age, that by geography and tradition has developed an individual way of life, and that his chief duty as an artist is to beautify, to purify and to enlarge that way of life.

R. S. Thomas, in *Wales,* no. 23, Autumn 1946

631   I think Wales should be proud of being the humblest country in the world.

Vernon Watkins, in *Wales*, no. 23, Autumn 1946

632   I am a Welshman with an international accent.

Arthur Horner, attributed in anonymous profile, in
The Welsh Review, vol. 6, no. 1, Spring 1947

633   The device of political expediency has served the Labour Party well in Wales.

Herbert Morrison MP, in speech in the House of Commons, 1947

634   The Welsh National spirit has had to bank itself up in the Welsh language for want of being able to express itself politically.

John Cowper Powys, *Obstinate Cymric*, 1947

635   It would be no gain whatsoever for English culture, for the Welsh, Scots and Irish to become indistinguishable from Englishmen – what *would* happen, of course, is that we should all become indistinguishable featureless 'Britons', at a lower level of culture than any of the separate regions. On the contrary, it is of great advantage for English culture to be constantly influenced from Scotland, Ireland and Wales.

T. S. Eliot, 'Unity and Diversity: the Region', *Notes Towards the Definition of Culture,* 1948

636   Towns are not typical of Wales, they are a manifestation of alien influences and the sooner they are scattered, the better.*

R. S. Thomas, 'Dau Gapel', in *Y Fflam*, May 1948

637   Unemployment was the evil that drove nearly half-a-million of our people from Wales between the two wars. It is the evil that breaks up our homes and our Welsh communities, and destroys our culture and our sense of nationhood.

S. O. Davies MP, in radio talk, 1949, in *Wales and the Wireless*, ed. Patrick Hannan, 1986

638   There is hardly a member of the present Government or of the Opposition who does not regard any insistence on the special claims and problems of Wales as an intolerable nuisance.

W. J. Gruffydd MP, 'Wales in Parliament', in *The Welsh Anvil*, vol. 1, no. 1, April 1949

639   We'll keep a welcome in the hillsides,
We'll keep a welcome in the vales,
This land you knew will still be singing
When you come home again to Wales.

This land of song will keep a welcome
And with a love that never fails,
We'll kiss away each hour of hiraeth
When you come home again to Wales.

Lyn Joshua and James Harper, 'We'll Keep a Welcome in the Hillsides', 1949

640　Why should I give a hang about Wales? It's by a mere fluke
of fate
That I live in its patch. On a map it does not rate

Higher than a scrap of earth in a back corner,
And a bit of a bother to those who believe in order.

And who is it lives in this spot, tell me that,
Who but the dregs of society? Please, cut it out,

This endless clatter of oneness and country and race:
You can get plenty of these, without Wales, any place.

I've long since had it with listening to the croon
Of the Cymry, indeed, forever moaning their tune.*
T. H. Parry-Williams, 'Hon'
(trans. Joseph P. Clancy), 1949

641　I feel the claws of Wales tearing at my heart.
God help me, I can't get away from this spot.*

642　Our aim will be to steel the will of our people for the
reconquest of Wales, for a free and independent Welsh People, for
the establishment of the Sovereign Independent Democratic
Republic of Wales.
editorial in *The Welsh Republican*, vol. 1, no. 1, August 1950

643　It is an insult to every Welshman to have flown in his
country the flag of the 'Union' effected by England, enforced by
England and maintained by England for England's gain, and
Wales's extinction.
Anonymous, 'What is the Union Jack?', in *The Welsh
Republican*, vol. 1, no. 2, October–November 1950

644　The Welsh eye needs to be educated.
Llewelyn Wyn Griffith, *The Welsh*, 1950

645　However numerous their faults and shortcomings, let it
always be remembered of the Welsh that the most widely popular
event of the year in Wales is a festival devoted to the Arts, and that
in it the highest form of tribute is reserved for poets. There is
nothing quite like it in the world.

646　There has been a distinct shift in Wales from *being* a peculiar nation to *saying* that we are a peculiar nation. Instead of talking Welsh as a matter of course, we now talk about being Welsh.

Richard Hughes, in radio talk, 1950, in Wales and the Wireless,
ed. Patrick Hannan, 1986

647   The influence of the BBC on the children of Wales is baneful.*

Kate Roberts, in Baner ac Amserau Cymru, 28 March 1950

648   To discuss the Conservative Party in relation to Welsh affairs is normally something of an extravagance.

editorial in The Welsh Republican, vol. 2, no. 3,
December 1951–January 1952.

649   A bookless people is a rootless people, doomed to lose its identity and its power of contributing to the common fund of civilization . . . If the published language goes, the language itself as a cultural medium will soon follow; and if Welsh goes, a bastardized vernacular will take its place.

The Ready Report on Publishing in Wales, 1951

650   Parochialism has been at least as much an evil in Wales as Anglicization, and local boy worship is an evil everywhere.

David Bell, 'Contemporary Welsh Painting', in
The Welsh Anvil, no. 3, July 1951

651   Wales has never had a wealthy, urban civilization, and it is unprofitable to suppose by claiming a few painters of Welsh birth and parentage as Welsh that there has ever been such a thing as Welsh painting.

652   Our exhortation to the people of Wales is to make use of every means they can to precipitate the crisis of England. In that crisis is the dawn of the new day that awaits the Welsh Nation.

Cliff Bere, 'The Way Forward', in The Welsh Republican, vol. 2,
no. 2, October–November 1951

653   Genuine English culture is rare in Wales, and rarest of all in the English-speaking areas.

Raymond Garlick, in editorial in Dock Leaves,
Michaelmas 1951

654   If there were six hundred angels in Westminster, they would

be English angels, and they would be unable to understand how Wales thinks.*

Cledwyn Hughes MP, in a speech at Parliament for Wales meeting in Caernarfon, reported in *Y Cymro*, 16 March 1951

655   The prevalence of Pacifism in Wales is but another manifestation of a slave mentality.

Mair Saunders Lewis, in *The Welsh Republican*, August–September 1951

656   Only too often has a Welshman's patriotism been a simmering stew of pacifism, sectarianism, teetotalism and chronic respectability.

657   Everyone will agree with this principle: safeguarding and ensuring the well-being of the Welsh language is more important for the nation of the Welsh than the winning of a Parliament for Wales . . . For the language can ensure the continuance of the nation; a Parliament cannot do that without the language.*

Saunders Lewis, in *Baner ac Amserau Cymru*, 20 June 1951

658   Some of us still believe that the great interpreter of Wales to the English . . . will yet come from the ranks of those who are fully within the mystery of our mother tongue.

A. G. Prys-Jones, 'Anglo-Welsh Poetry Today', in *The British Weekly,* 22 February 1951

659   There is in the Welsh language raw material as lasting in the true craftsman's hands as were the marble-quarries of Greece and Italy in times gone by.*

D. J. Williams, in adjudication at the National Eisteddfod, August 1951

660   Toryism is the enemy which is murdering Wales. Our answer must be to rise and destroy it in Wales. We will make Wales an untenable position for it under whatever camouflage it tries to remain; we will drive it back into its own land from every entrenchment it has made in our country and in our minds; we will show that Wales belongs not to England, but to the world.

Cliff Bere, *The Welsh Republic*, 1952

661   I wanted to save the Rhondda valley for the nation
      and the nation itself as a fertile garden.*

J. Kitchener Davies, 'Sŵn y Gwynt sy'n Chwythu', 1952

662   ... the cancer of Englishness that is twisting through
Wales.*

663   One of the great advantages of living in a small country, as
we in Wales know, is that nearly everybody knows everybody else
– or at least his cousin.
Raymond Garlick, in editorial in *Dock Leaves*, vol. 3, no. 9,
Winter 1952

664   We were a people bred on legends,
Warming our hands at the red past . . .
We were a people wasting ourselves
In fruitless battles for our masters,
In lands to which we had no claim,
With men for whom we felt no hatred . . .
We were a people, and are so yet.
When we have finished quarrelling for crumbs
Under the table, or gnawing the bones
Of a dead culture, we will arise,
Armed, but not in the old way.
R. S. Thomas, 'Welsh History', 1952

665   There is no present in Wales,
And no future;
There is only the past,
Brittle with relics,
Wind-bitten towers and castles
With sham ghosts;
Mouldering quarries and mines;
And an impotent people,
Sick with inbreeding,
Worrying the carcase of an old song.
R. S. Thomas, 'Welsh Landscape', 1952

666   Although those of us who have been brought up in Monmouth and Glamorgan are not Welsh-speaking, Welsh-writing
Welshmen, nevertheless we are all aware of the fact that there
exists in Wales, and especially in the rural areas, a culture which is
unique in the world. And we are not prepared to see it die.
Aneurin Bevan, in speech in the House of Commons during
Welsh Day debate, 12 December 1953

667   The role of the Anglo-Welsh writer is the translator's role. He
lives on his grandmother's memories, and attempts to translate them

into a language which she knew not. We are allowed the luxury of
the 'Anglo' because some people remain stubbornly Welsh.

Aneirin Talfan Davies, 'A Question of Language', in
The Welsh Anvil, no. 5, July 1953

668 Pay a penny for my singing torch,
O my sisters, my brothers of the land of my mothers,
The land of our fathers, our troubles, our dreams,
The land of Llewellyn and Shoni bach Shinkin,
The land of the sermons that pebble the streams,
The land of the englyn and Crawshay's old engine,
The land that is sometimes as proud as she seems.

Idris Davies, 'Land of my Mothers', 1953

669 The University is by far the most effective instrument we
have in Wales for bringing the different parts of the country
together and healing the divisions between North and South which
the geography of Wales, powerfully allied with British railways
and our road system, have done so much to create.

Sir Emrys Evans, in speech to the Court of the University
College of North Wales, Bangor, November 1953

670 To say merely that the Welsh tongue has survived is to give a
wrong emphasis . . . It is no petrified tree dug from the bogs of
time but a flowering shrub.

Thomas Firbank, *A Country of Memorable Honour*, 1953

671 The obvious answer to those who attack the National
Eisteddfod because Anglo-Welsh writers cannot participate is that
all these objectors should start a festival of their own. There is no
reason at all why they should not: all that is required is the
initiative and the capital – which, one trusts, the newspapers which
attack the all-Welsh rule would readily provide.

Raymond Garlick, in editorial in *Dock Leaves*,
vol. 4, no. 12, Winter 1953

672 The Anglo-Welsh have had no major literary critic, nor even
a responsible second-rate critic of talent. There have been bootless
discussions of whether they were Anglo or Welsh . . . and frequent
mutual back-scratching. But the main problem, their function as a
bulwark of civilization against suburban conformity, and their
relationship to the community which has reared them, and its
traditions, have been only superficially dealt with.

Bobi Jones, 'The Anglo-Welsh', in *Dock Leaves*, vol. 3, no. 10,
Spring 1953

673   If any system of justice is to be respected in Wales it must deal with us as men with the right to the administration of justice in our own tongue, and not as rascals who will ere long, by the grace of further education and government, attain the status of civilized, monoglot Englishmen.
R. Tudur Jones, in editorial in *Welsh Nation*, June 1953

674   We have lost the most splendid English-speaking child Wales has produced for centuries, and at a time when he had an abundance of plans for the future. Let perpetual light shine upon him.
Saunders Lewis, in a tribute to Dylan Thomas, broadcast in the Welsh Home Service, 10 November 1953

675   What is surprising is the permanence and persistence of the Welsh way of life and belief, an intense cultural and intellectual conservatism which shows itself sometimes in an almost Chinese reverence for what is established and sanctified by custom, a strange form of ancestor worship which is all the stranger because, as an articulate body of thought and belief, it is not more than a hundred and fifty years old.
Goronwy Rees, in radio talk, 1953, in *Wales and the Wireless*, ed. Patrick Hannan, 1986

676   Is there no passion in Wales?
R. S. Thomas, 'The Minister', 1953

677   Protestantism – the adroit castrator
      Of art; the bitter negation
      Of song and dance and the heart's innocent joy –
      You have botched our flesh and left us only the soul's
      Terrible impotence in a warm world.

678   If it may be said that there is a divine right to anything on earth, the right over the land of Wales belongs to the Welsh nation, and not to any alien, whoever he may be.*
D. J. Williams, *Yr Hen Dŷ Fferm* (trans. Waldo Williams), 1953

679   Fundamentally, asking for our own parliament for our own affairs is a simple matter of self-respect, not one of throwing our might about and clamouring for preferential treatment. It is for us to decide, one way or another, whether Wales is to become extinct. A Parliament of its own won't in itself guarantee the future, but we shall at least have the means to settle our own affairs. The question

to which we must await an answer is whether sufficient of us want a Wales with a future to it.

G. O. Williams, 'Why demand a Parliament?', in *Dock Leaves*,
vol. 4, no. 12, Winter 1953

680   There are those who put their finger on an infinitesimal part of the whole and say, That is *my* Wales, the *true* Wales; so expelling the rest to a limbo beyond concern.

681   One hears the wind moaning through the ruins of a ruined habitation when one hears a Welsh place-name on the tongues of people to whom it means nothing.

Waldo Williams, 'Anglo-Welsh and Welsh', in *Dock Leaves*,
vol. 4, no. 12, Winter 1953

682   The Wales of today is not a unity. There is not one Wales; there are three Wales. There is Welsh Wales; there is industrial, or as I sometimes think of it, American Wales; and there is upper-class or English Wales.

Alfred E. Zimmern, *My Impressions of Wales*, 1953

683   To call the Eisteddfod's leaders fanatical is not to their discredit; a fanatical desire to enhance the culture of Wales is no subject for disapproval.

editorial in *Western Mail*, 8 April 1954

684   We share the deep concern that is felt by the Welsh people for the preservation of our language and the heritage of our cultural life. We shall strive to assist every effort to preserve this precious heritage. The Labour members of Parliament for Wales have been reared in the best traditions of our country. We are inheritors of the social democracy which is the characteristic of the valleys and the countryside. We are determined that we shall play our part in sustaining the heritage which has come down to us.

James Griffiths MP, in statement after conference at Llanelli,
15 March 1954

685   Within the whispering gallery of St Paul's
The merest whisper travels round the walls;
But in the parts where I was born and bred
Folk hear things long before they're even said.

A. G. Prys-Jones, 'Quite So', 1954

686   Praise the Lord! We are a musical nation.

Revd Eli Jenkins,
in Dylan Thomas, *Under Milk Wood*, 1954

687   I must regretfully believe that our Welsh language, having fulfilled its purpose and controlled by inexorable laws of the universe, must in this technological age, just fade away.

Mrs Williams Doo, in *Liverpool Daily Post*, 15 February 1954

688   He sounded like an actor pretending, with fair success on the whole, to be Owain Glyndŵr in a play on the Welsh Children's Hour.

Kingsley Amis, *That Uncertain Feeling*, 1955

689   What a disgrace it was, what a reproach to all Welshmen, that so many of the articulate parts of their culture should be invalidated by awful sentimental lying. All those phoney novels and stories about the wry rhetorical wisdom of poetical miners, all those boring myths about the wonder and the glory and the terror of life in the valley towns, all those canonizations of literary deadbeats, charlatans and flops – all this in a part of the world where there was enough material to keep a hundred honest poets and novelists chained to the typewriter.

690   It's standard practice, of course, with writers of Probert's allegiance, to pretend to be wild valley babblers, woaded with pit-dirt and sheep-shit, thinking in Welsh the whole time and obsessed with terrible beauty etc. but in fact they tend to come from comfortable middle-class homes, have a good urban education, never go near a lay-preacher and couldn't even order a pint in Welsh.

691   Wales is our share of the human crisis.*

Ambrose Bebb, 'Diweddglo', *Yr Argyfwng*, 1955

692   *All* sorts come from Cardiff.

Love Pritchard, the 'King' of Bardsey, quoted in
Mortimer Wheeler, *Still Digging*, 1955

693   The essential genius of Wales is social. Welsh warmth and comradeship could make nationalization and the welfare state something more than bureaucracy and turn code-numbers back into human beings.

Ioan Bowen Rees, quoted in *News Chronicle*, 21 December 1955

694   One: I am a Welshman; two: I am a drunkard; three: I am a lover of the human race, especially of women.

> Dylan Thomas, attributed by Geoffrey Moore in
> *The Kenyon Review*, Spring 1955

695   Land of my Fathers. My fathers can keep it.

> attributed by Suzanne Roussillat, in *Adam*, 23 December 1955

696   Welsh is of this soil, this island, the senior language of the men of Britain; and Welsh is beautiful.

> J. R. R. Tolkien, *The O'Donnell Lecture*, 1955

697   Apart from a handsome civic centre, the streets of Cardiff seemed unbearably mean and dingy, the people in them unbelievably foreign and barbaric.

> Mortimer Wheeler, *Still Digging*, 1955

698   Wales, save when united in opposition to England, was an aggregate of parish pumps rather than a nation.

699   What we know of the Welsh seems mighty little, compared with what we think we know of the Scotch or Irish. An invidious nursery rhyme; some lampooning, not without rough admiration, in Shakespeare; what else? A contumacious people, the Cymri, confederates never any longer than they had to be, fighting with, and beaten by Romans, Saxons, Normans, Danes, Irish, turning around, as often as not, and mauling their oppressors, coming home victorious, to betray their leaders and fall to feuding, repeating the cycle.

> Rolfe Humphries, *Green Armor on Green Ground*, 1956

700   Wales, which I have never seen,
Is gloomy, mountainous, and green.

> 'For my Ancestors', in *Green Armor on Green Ground*

701   In me Wales is one.*

> Waldo Williams, 'Cymru'n Un', in *Dail Pren*, 1956

702   What is being a nation? A talent
Springing from the heart.
And love of country? Keeping house
Among a cloud of witnesses.*

> 'Pa beth yw Dyn?' (trans. Emyr Humphreys)

703 The Anglo-Welsh now have a literature.

Gwyn Jones, *The First Forty Years*, 1957

704 The Anglo-Welsh, though they are a danger to the Welsh language, must never be its enemy; and the Welsh Welsh, even if they are the true dancers before our tribal ark, will be unwise to try to impose an irresistible logic upon an immovable fact; they must accept that they cannot speak for, or even to, half their fellow-countrymen, while to the great world outside they may not speak at all.

705 Perhaps we are doomed always to be a People of the Short Puff, stricken with the trembles beyond a middle distance, and with gripes, grunts and staggers after the vital sixth round. Deft assemblers of the house of one night, but lacking the architectonics for castles or cathedrals.

706 'Anglo-Welsh', after all, is just a tag, a literary label, a device for avoiding circumlocution.

707 The majority of the Anglo-Welsh have been quite painfully modest and deferential in face of native Welsh criticism: we would no more talk back to a proper Cymro than we would cheek our mother.

708 Welsh is a brave language and cannot be spoken mincingly or through immobile lips.

Elwyn Davies, *A Gazetteer of Welsh Place-names*, 1958

709 [The] survival of something which has an unbroken tradition in this island since the end of the sixth century, and which embodies deposits far older still, cannot be regarded as a matter of indifference by any person claiming to care for the things of this island. It is by no means a matter for the Welsh only, but concerns us all, because the complex and involved heritage of Britain is a shared inheritance which can, in very devious ways, enrich us all.

David Jones, in letter to *The Times*, 11 June 1958, in *Epoch and Artist*, 1959

710 A foreigner could spend a week in Cardiff or Penarth and think himself still in England.

James Morris, 'Welshness in Wales', in *Wales*, September 1958

711 When an Englishman has a pint too many, he wants to fight, or make love, or subside into the womb of smutty anecdote; but

when the Welshman stands beside the bar he, apparently, wants to sing.

712   In general, therefore, Welsh is the language of the illiterate Welsh, English of the literate Welsh.

> Lord Raglan, 'I take my stand', in *Wales*, October 1958

713   Ebbw Vale is in England.

714   There are still parts of Wales where the only concession to gaiety is a striped shroud.

> Gwyn Thomas, in *Punch*, 18 June 1958

715   We who desire peace and goodwill before all else in life must deeply deplore this modern obsession with our language. We believe it to be on the side of those forces that lead to war.

> Mrs Williams Doo, in *Western Mail*, 24 October 1958

716   There is no more noble sight than that of a Welshman and an Englishman facing one another across a pint of simple beer, each aware of the other's failings – laying their cards on the table with that cool intellectuality which so characterizes the relationship between the two races; smilingly tolerant, so glad that a common frontier, with no passport difficulties, has made them, with all their differences, so understanding of one another.

> Gareth Lloyd Evans, 'How to Live in England', in *Wales,* no. 40, May 1959

717   The ideas of our professional politicians as to what can be done for Wales are vague, obscure and tentative. Their views upon what cannot be done for her are clear and strong.

> Gwynfor Evans, 'Wales as an Economic Entity', in *Wales*, nos. 42/44, September 1959

718   The greatest tragedy which has happened in Wales in the twentieth century has been the establishment of the Welsh Nationalist Party.

> Emlyn Hooson MP, in speech in the House of Commons, 23 May 1959

719   All the masters [at Llandovery College] were from English public schools and they never let us forget their opinion of our native inferiority, from which our only hope of redemption was through emulating the *Herrenvolk* whose outposts they were.

> Ernest Jones, *Free Associations*, 1959

720 A Welshman writing in English only acquires significance when he is seen to be inextricably committed to and involved in the predicament of his country.

Harri Webb, in *Wales*, no. 46, November 1959

721 Wales has had enough inspired ignoramuses to last her till Doomsday; what we need is a drop of the old culture, with its grace that is only gained by a great deal of hard work.

Anthony Conran, 'The English Poet in Wales', in *The Anglo-Welsh Review*, vol. 10, no. 26, 1960

722 The Arts Council mentality
Minces in teashops, talks glibly of
Striking a blow for Wales – five more minutes
In Welsh on the Welsh BBC.

Anthony Conran, 'An Invocation of Angels', 1960

723 A Welshman at twenty
Is either an awkward edition of fifty
Or else he's gone English.

724 All this play-acting about Wales doesn't matter, boy. Wales is just another country like any other.

Captain John Roberts,
in Alun Owen, *After the Funeral*, 1960

725 In my experience of funerals in Wales, everybody wants something. Death's a great time for grabbing the left-overs, my boy. An acre, a sow, an old engagement ring.

726 The shape of Wales: pig-headed, you say, to remember to draw it.

Raymond Williams, *Border Country*, 1960

727 No language can be restored by a language movement. It can be restored only by a movement which reaches down to the deep sources of a people's will. The Welsh language can be saved only by a great national revival directed to securing full nationhood for Wales.

Gwynfor Evans, in *Celtic Voice*, vol. 1, 1961

728 Immerse yourself in the literature of your language. Give yourself up to it as far as you are able. Everything else is of secondary importance. To be in the fashion and to follow the

fashions of London or Paris are wholly secondary in comparison with knowing your Welsh tradition.*

Saunders Lewis, advice to a young writer, in conversation with
Aneirin Talfan Davies, broadcast by the BBC, 19 May 1960, in
Taliesin, no. 2, Christmas 1961

729   I had a desire, no small desire, a great desire to change the history of Wales. To change the entire course of Wales, and make Welsh Wales something alive, strong, powerful, belonging to the modern world. And I failed utterly.*

730   They can be pretty rough, them Taffies, if they put their mind to it.

Ted,
in Alun Owen, *Lena, Oh my Lena*, 1961

731   Even God had a Welsh name:
      We spoke to him in the old language;
      He was to have a peculiar care
      For the Welsh people.

R. S. Thomas, 'A Welsh Testament', 1961

732   I find
      This hate's for my own kind,
      For men of the Welsh race
      Who brood with dark face
      Over their thin navel
      To learn what to sell.

733   I like to think of Swansea as a place with no sophistication, no cultural props, no reputation of any kind. A hidden place.

Vernon Watkins, in radio talk, 1961,
in *Wales and the Wireless*, ed. Patrick Hannan, 1986

734   Rural Wales is where I belong, but I don't want to live in it, I want to have it to go back to.

Emlyn Williams, *George*, 1961

735   It will be nothing less than a revolution to restore the Welsh language in Wales today. Success is only possible through revolutionary methods. Perhaps the language would bring self-government in its wake – I don't know. The language is more important than self-government. *

Saunders Lewis, *Tynged yr Iaith*, 1962

736 I predict that Welsh as a living language will cease to be, if present trends continue, about the beginning of the twenty-first century, supposing that there are still men alive in Britain then.*

737 In Wales all can be forgiven except being serious about the language.*

738 In my opinion, if any kind of self-government were obtained before the Welsh language was acknowledged and used as an official language in local authority and state administration in the Welsh-speaking parts of our country, then the language would never achieve official status at all, and its demise would be quicker than it will be under English rule.*

739 Laugharne was the town of Dylan Thomas, the Welsh poet who in his short days on earth was as much a wizard as Merlin, a man who climbed a unique throne of love and laughter, and died from the sheer height of it . . . At his worst, he traversed some most peculiar valleys of disgrace. At his best, he lit up a whole new sky of delight, put to shame some of the darker absurdities of our serge-bound consciences and added to the Anglo-Welsh tongue a new dimension of lovely sound.

Gwyn Thomas, in *TV Times*, 14 September 1962

740 The future of Wales depends on young people who have the ability to draft a good amendment, not on those who can handle high explosives.

Cledwyn Hughes MP, 'The Importance of Welsh Water', in
Liverpool Daily Post, 26 April 1963

741 Always I feel the cold and cutting blast
Of winds that blow about my native hills,
And know that I can never be content
In this or any other continent
Until with my frosty fathers I am at last
Back in the old country that sings and kills.

T. H. Jones, 'Land of my Fathers', 1963

742 The Welsh language is the only weapon which can supplant English government in Wales.*

Saunders Lewis, in *Barn*, March 1963

743   There is only one true patriotism: that which sees the homeland as it really is and loves it nevertheless.

> Meic Stephens, 'The Matter with Wales', in *The Nationalist*,
> vol. 1, no. 1, June 1963

744   I hope it will not be long before the people of Wales realise
that, although the dead are always with us, the walking dead can
sometimes be avoided.

745   The Welsh are too fond of waving rhetorical flags of
defiance while preparing for the expected defeat.

746   Let's be kind to Anglo-Saxons,
        To our neighbours let's be nice,
      Welshmen, put aside all hatred,
        Learn to love the bloody Sais!

> Meic Stephens, 'Our English Friends', 1963

747   I tried to interpret the dreams of a people who didn't know
they were asleep.

> Gwyn Thomas, *Jackie the Jumper*, 1963

748   Seeing how Wales fares
      Now, I will attend rather
      To things as they are; to green grass
      That is not ours; to visitors
      Buying us up. Thousands of mouths
      Are emptying their waste speech
      About us, and an Elsan culture
      Threatens us.

> R. S. Thomas, 'Looking at Sheep', 1963

749   Cold water, Dewi,
      Is not for our palate,
      We keep your festival
      With foolish mirth,
      Self-praise and self-pity,
      Dragons and flagons,
      But none who will suffer
      For Wales in her dearth.

> Harri Webb, 'Tŷ Ddewi', 1963

750   Wales is older than the British Empire, and she will live long
after it, too.*

> D. J. Williams, *AE a Chymru*, 1963

751   Another idiotic creation is the Department for Wales, a completely new office for Jim Griffiths and his two parliamentary secretaries, all the result of a silly election pledge.

> Richard Crossman, entry in diary, 1964, in
> *The Crossman Diaries*, 1979

752   Wales is a small country and the Welsh are a small people.

> Goronwy Rees, 'Have the Welsh a Future?', in
> *Encounter*, March 1964

753   The Welsh are a peace-loving people with a profound respect for established authority. It is not likely that Welsh Gandhis or Welsh gunmen will ever set the hearts of their countrymen aflame.

754   The Welsh answer to a problem is nearly always to appoint a committee.

755   Wales until today has lived so long upon its past that it has offered very little to the young imagination, handcuffed and fettered in the narrow world of the chapel and the Eisteddfod.

756   The Nonconformist chapels which have exerted so decisive an influence on every aspect of Welsh life are today empty or emptying; faith has ebbed away from them, and in Wales as elsewhere, television now has more influence than religion.

757   It is a mark of the sterility of the official version of Welsh culture that it has never succeeded in giving any adequate expression to the kind of society which flourished in the South Wales valleys.

758   We were not, in terms of nationality, a homogenous people. Into the valleys had poured as many Englishmen as indigenous Welsh. The only binding things were indignity and deprivation. The Welsh language stood in the way of our fuller union and we made ruthless haste to destroy it. We nearly did.

> Gwyn Thomas, *A Welsh Eye*, 1964

759   The price of a pound of beef is more important than your bloody language.

> George Brown MP, in speech at Bangor, 1965

760   What is Welshness? It is a wine you can never chill, a welcome you can seldom outstay. It is warmth and homeliness and concern and gregariousness and a kindliness which will dissemble rather than hurt. It is a sense of friendship with all men, born of closely shared danger and privation and deprivation in farming and mining and quarrying communities. It is small-mindedness, too, and a sense of inferiority and much, much more. But whatever else it is, with hand on heart and heart on sleeve, it is passionate because the one extravagance of the Welsh is words, and their abiding passion is literacy.

Hywel Davies, in BBC lunch-time lecture, 1965

761   The plain truth is this: the majority of Welsh-speakers will never ask for forms and documents in their own language . . . It will take two generations to teach the Welsh-speaking Welsh to use their language in oral and written form without shame and fear.*

Islwyn Ffowc Elis, in editorial in *Taliesin*,
vol. 11, December 1965

762   Alas, there is one sad difference between the Welsh Nationalist Party of the 1960s and the Welsh Methodists of the 1760s. The Methodists in their day aroused hate, violence, persecution, prison. That is why they triumphed.

Saunders Lewis, 'Welsh Literature and Nationalism', in
Western Mail, 13 March 1965

763   Civilization must be more than an abstraction. It must have 'a local habitation and a name'. Here, its name is Wales.

764   Rugby, as played by the Welsh, is not a game. It is a tribal mystery.

Gwyn Thomas, 'Padded up for Action', in *A Hatful of Humours*, 1965

765   If people want to sing, dance, become crowned bards and dress up in night-shirts, why not? It's just that it means so much to some people and so little to others. In my particular neck of the woods, it falls far short of 'Come Dancing' and the International Horse Show in terms of appeal.

Herbert Williams, in *South Wales Echo*, 1965

766   Of course I'd go back if somebody'd pay me
       To live in my own country
       Like a bloody Englishman.

T. H. Jones, 'Back?', 1965

767 I am as keen as anyone on the due preservation of the language but many of these fanatics are dancing around the language like a lot of old-time Cherokee Indians around a totempole. In fact, they are making a laughing-stock of the language in the rest of the United Kingdom.

> Lord Ogmore, reported in *Western Mail*, 14 December 1966

768 There can be few parts of Britain where enthusiasm for the arts gutters as tremulously as in South Wales.

> Gwyn Thomas, 'Plaster Saints in the Valleys', in
> *Twentieth Century*, Winter 1966

769 Cardiff contains without question the least intelligent part of the Welsh proletariat, for the simple reason that it is in no sense Welsh.

770 The Welsh Arts Council mounts brilliant skirmishes.

771 Most of the effects of organized religion I have seen in Wales: the sly malignity of interdenominational intrigue; the gross persecution of beauty and delight by diaconates delirious with some phobic sense of guilt.

772 I think it is quite clear that the proper language for court proceedings in Wales is the English language.

> Justice Widgery, in the Royal Court of Justice,
> 9 December 1966

773 Oh yes, there have been gains.
I merely state
That the old language, for us,
Is part of the old, abandoned ways.
And when I hear it, regret
Disturbs me like a requiem.

> Herbert Williams, 'The Old Tongue', 1966

774 If Welsh dies the loss to the nation would be incalculable. A language represents the consciousness of a nation and is a safeguard of its individual identity. If we let that die, then perhaps a part of us will die too.

> editorial in *Western Mail*, 8 June 1967

775 In any legal proceeding in Wales or Monmouthshire the Welsh language may be spoken by any party, witness or other

person who desires to use it, subject in the case of proceedings in a court other than a magistrates' court to such prior notice as may be required by rules of court; and any necessary provision for interpretation shall be made accordingly.

The Welsh Language Act, 1967

776   Wales was *given* to us, the English *made* England.*
R. T. Jenkins, *Clywed yr Hyfrydlais*, 1967

777   Talking about national issues is the Welsh equivalent of sore-scratching: it affords temporary relief from the problems involved without moving any nearer to a cure.
Gerald Morgan, 'More of the Dragon's Tongue', in
Welsh Dominion, no. 1, Summer 1967

778   The first task of the new critics will be to distinguish Welsh literature in English from work in the main stream of English literature which just happens to have been written by someone qualified by birth, residence or parentage to play rugby for Wales, or just happens to have a background of Welsh place-names.
Ioan Bowen Rees, in letter to Meic Stephens, in *Poetry Wales*,
vol. 3, no. 2, Summer 1967

779   Anglo-Welsh literature is a recent phenomenon. It has its roots in newly disturbed soil – the social and linguistic upheaval that occurred in Wales during the inter-war years.
Meic Stephens, 'The Second Flowering', in *Poetry Wales*,
vol. 3, no. 3, Winter 1967–8

780   The big danger threatening Anglo-Welsh verse, as I see it, is that it is and may continue to be peripheral, both in Wales and in England . . . While so many of us acquiesce in the anglo-centric organization of life in Britain today, I think our literature will remain in the same position as Scotland's before its renaissance in the nineteen twenties: parochial, disorientated, minor, conservative, dull, and without one poet, or a critic, of Hugh MacDiarmid's stature.

781   Whether we are likely to flourish and create a literature that measures up to European standards is not yet clear. The only alternative, for me, is that, with the Welsh nation denied the rights and responsibilities of full nationhood, a parliament at least, and therefore obliterated by the end of the present century, the Welsh will have lost their separate identity and the Anglo-Welsh will then

have nothing to distinguish them from other regional English writers.

782   The influence of R. S. Thomas is, of course, much in evidence here but his brooding on rural decay and the spineless attitudes of his countrymen may well prove to be an emotional dead end, however salutary for the time being.

783   I have lived where blood
Had flowed down men's hands.
Though I look for a Wales
Free as the Netherlands,
A freedom hacked out here
Is a freedom without worth,
A terror without beauty.
Here it must come to birth
Not as a pterodactyl
Flailing archaic wings,
But the dove that broods on chaos –
Wise as a thousand springs.

Raymond Garlick, 'Matters Arising', 1968

784   The English pound makes much the same snarl in Wales as anywhere else in these islands and I have not yet happened on anyone, poet or otherwise, who scorns its definitive crackle.

Peter Gruffydd, 'Further to the Second Flowering', in
Poetry Wales, vol. 4, no. 1, Summer 1968

785   I would like Anglo-Welsh writers to see themselves first as Welshmen. The only English thing about an Anglo-Welsh writer ought to be his language.

Glyn Jones, *The Dragon Has Two Tongues*, 1968

786   To me, anyone can be a Welshman who chooses to be so and is prepared to take the consequences.

787   I should remain committed to Wales even if I were certain that within ten years Wales would be finished.*

Saunders Lewis, 'Treiswyr sy'n ei chipio hi', in *Barn*,
no. 74, December 1968

788   The battle for Wales is the battle for all small nations, all small communities, all individuals in the age of genocide.

Ioan Bowen Rees, *Celtic Nationalism*, 1968

789   It is intolerable that those who do not speak Welsh should be regarded as second-class citizens, or less genuine lovers of their country than their bilingual counterparts. But it is equally intolerable that in their own country or Church those who speak or think in Welsh should be regarded as eccentric or perverse or expected in matters governmental or official to be provided with forms in a language in which they are not at home.

Glyn Simon, reported in *Western Mail*, 26 September 1968

790   I have walked the shore
For an hour and seen the English
Scavenging among the remains
Of our culture, covering the sand
Like the tide and, with the roughness
Of the tide, elbowing our language
Into the grave that we have dug for it.

R. S. Thomas, 'Reservoirs', 1968

791   Where can I go, then, from the smell
Of decay, from the putrefying of a dead
Nation?

792   I wouldn't have anything to do with politics if Wales were a healthy little country like other free countries.*

D. J. Williams, in radio talk, 1968, in *Radio Cymru*, ed. Gwyn Erfyl, 1989

793   We call upon Welshmen to organize, train and equip, to arm themselves with guns, bombs, Molotov cocktails, grenades, pikes, bows and arrows, swords, bayonets, clubs . . . eggs filled with sand, flour and smoke bombs, nuts and bolts, sharpened pennies . . . Stock them up and bring them to Caernarfon.

in leaflet distributed by the Free Wales Army prior to the investiture of the Prince of Wales, July 1969

794   Having spent so many hours in the language laboratory here I shall certainly never let it [the Welsh language] die without offering stout resistance.

Charles, Prince of Wales, in a speech at the Urdd Eisteddfod, reported in *Western Mail*, 2 June 1969

795   It's sweet to be a Welshman
And to paint the world green.*

Robat Gruffudd, *I'r Chwyldro*, 1969

796   Welsh literature is the major achievement of the Welsh
nation and the most complete expression of the Welsh mind
through the centuries.

Bobi Jones, *Highlights in Welsh Literature*, 1969

797   The young writer in Welsh today is consciously building up
the nerve of his community, and slowly healing a deep and ancient
wound.

798   If we are tempted to think that Welsh language extremists
are inexcusable, let us remember that the threats to the survival of
Welsh have never, either quantitatively or qualititatively, been
greater than they are today. A note of desperation in its defenders
should surely be understood and excused.

Glyn Simon, reported in *Western Mail*, 1 March 1969

799   In the striped flag
      On the tower there is the insolence
      Of a poster advertising
      A nation for sale.

R. S. Thomas, 'Shame', 1969

800   Two lands at last connected
      Across the waters wide,
      And all the tolls collected
      On the English side.

Harri Webb, 'Ode to the Severn Bridge', 1969

801   This futile bird, it seems to me,
      Would make a perfect Welsh MP

Harri Webb, 'Our Budgie', 1969

802   One day, when Wales is free and prosperous
      And dull, they'll all be wishing they were us.

Harri Webb, 'Merlin's Prophecy 1969', 1969

803   Never forget your Welsh.

advertisement for beer, 1970

804   Happiness is knowing you are Welsh.

car-sticker, 1970

805   We must not forget that the main cause of the decline in the
Welsh language is that not enough Welsh mothers see value in

bringing up their children as Welsh-speakers. Acts which tend to associate the language with law-breaking and rebelliousness are not, in my view, going to encourage these mothers. What is needed is more constructive work directed at showing that ability to speak Welsh as well as English is an asset of real cultural and vocational use.

Sir Goronwy Daniel, First Impressions of the
University Scene, 1970

806 The Welsh condition is worth studying because it is spreading.

Emyr Humphreys, 'The Welsh Condition', in The Spectator,
28 March 1970

807 If ambition and wealth and power are the highest ventures, then obviously he [the young Welshman] must strike out into a wider world and take the path of Henry Tudor and David Lloyd George. On the other hand, if he wishes to take up a cause, if he feels a deep sense of loyalty to the community which nurtured him, if he wishes to work out his salvation in fear and trembling, if he sets a high price on honour and personal integrity, or if he is just a high-minded humanist, there is more than enough scope for his talents in Wales itself.

808 While accepting that . . . economic developments and the pressure of circumstances have hastened the decline of Welsh, yet somewhere at the heart of the whole business there was a will at work. The destruction of our identity was willed by the power which usurped our sovereignty.*

J. R. Jones, Ac Onide, 1970

809 We have no existence as a rightful people . . . except through the inter-penetration of our dwelling-place, 'this corner of the earth', with the Welsh language.*

810 It is said of one experience that it is among the most agonizing of all . . . namely, that of having to leave the soil of your country for ever, of turning your back on your heritage, of being torn away by the roots from your homeland. . . . I have not suffered that experience. But I know of another which is just as painful, and more irreversible (for one can always return to one's home), and that is the experience of knowing, not that you are leaving your country, but that your country is leaving you, is ceasing to exist under your very feet, is being sucked away from you, as if by an insatiable,

consuming wind, into the hands and possession of another country and another civilization.*

J. R. Jones, *Gwaedd yng Nghymru*, 1970

811 Perhaps I have a suspicious mind, but the south Wales valleys breed suspicious minds.

Neil Kinnock MP, in maiden speech in the House of Commons,
13 July 1970

812 We are not asking for the moon. We are asking for our own radio and television channels.

Emyr Llewelyn, 'The Future of Broadcasting', in *Planet*,
no. 2, October/November 1970

813 Welsh? I have never heard such rubbish!

Justice Edward Rowley, on refusing permission for defendants to speak
Welsh in court, reported in *Western Mail*, 12 December 1970

814 Mr George Thomas [Secretary of State for Wales] spoke of the language as of a rejected wife – with deliberate goodwill, no love, and periodic complaints about what it was costing him.

Ned Thomas, 'The George Thomas Era', in *Planet,*
no. 1, August/September 1970

815 During the George Thomas era the battle for moral leadership in Wales was gradually lost, and the lessons of this time need a lot of thinking over by Welshmen who call themselves Socialists.

816 In the long term it is the interaction of socialism and nationalism that will decide the future of this corner of the world, and what sort of socialism and what sort of nationalism, are important questions for us. Devolution is a subject that can be phrased either in terms of national rights or socialist rights. It scarcely matters which.

817 The Welsh language has become in both senses a club: it is a conspiracy of people seeking preferment through the speaking of an arcane tongue; it is an offensive weapon for use against the British Government.

Gwyn Thomas, entry in journal, 1970

818 The visitor to North Wales should remember that, in architecture as in other matters, English standards do not apply.

Elizabeth Beasley, *The Shell Guide to North Wales*, 1971

819   Parochialism is of the mind; the Welsh language is of Europe and of the world.

Pennar Davies, in *Artists in Wales*, ed. Meic Stephens, 1971

820   I find it difficult to accept the genuineness of any concern for Wales professed by those who see London as the centre of their political activities and aspirations. The first condition of the very survival of our people is that there should be a psychological coming home to Wales, in political and economic matters as in others, and that those of our countrymen who call themselves socialists and radicals and democrats should see in Wales the proposed centre for the implementation of their principles.

821   To live in Wales
         is to love sheep
         and be afraid
         of dragons.

Peter Finch, 'A Welsh Wordscape', 1971

822   I oppose the leaders of Plaid Cymru because they are prepared to sacrifice their people, their country and their heritage on the shrine of their respectability and pacifism.

John Jenkins, in a letter from prison, in *Planet*,
nos. 5/6, Summer 1971

823   She [Wales] is not a beautiful young girl after whom I lust, or an old duchess whose money and status I desire; she is old, well past her best, decrepit, boozy, and has taken strange bedfellows without the saving grace of desperation . . . I owe her my love and loyalty, she is my mother.

824   Wales will not be Wales without the Welsh language. Without the language strongly rooted in its soil, it would be another country, and because of this, there is only one battle worth fighting in the Wales of today. And that is the language battle, the battle to bring it back to the *totality* of the life of Wales.*

Saunders Lewis, in *Barn*, February 1971

825   Only out of free choice can there be built a Wales in English which is not England and which is in touch with the living heart of a Wales that beats in Welsh.

Roland Mathias, in *Artists in Wales*, ed. Meic Stephens, 1971

826   It is indeed a depressing experience now to move about the

cultural void which is English-speaking Wales, to discover how totally ignorant of Welsh history and tradition its people are and how superficially unconcerned about it, and to observe the absence of leadership in the necessary quantity and quality from universities and schools.

827   As to whether I am Welsh or not, it is a highly self-conscious question which I have never felt the need to ask myself. *I am.* It is enough, and the rest is propaganda.

Alun Richards, in *Artists in Wales*, ed. Meic Stephens, 1971

828   People will not understand that a language which has had no utility in our lives is unlikely to be of importance to us ever again.

829   Nothing irritates English-speaking areas in Wales more than bilingual forms.

George Thomas MP, reported in *Liverpool Daily Post*,
20 April 1971

830   I am a Welsh aristocrat. In a good light I can trace my ancestry all the way back to my father.

Gwyn Thomas, entry in journal, 1971

831   The Red Dragon, to the bemused ear of the valley-dweller, could as well refer to a beer or a bus as a flag.

832   Cardiff wants to be seen to be a capital; it doesn't want to act like one.

Ned Thomas, 'I will cling to the old Celtic cross', in *Planet*,
no. 7, October/November 1971

833   Very soon there will be no quiet, comfortable way left of being a Welsh-speaking Welshman; traditional Welshness seems more and more a sham. We either have to lie down as if dead or do something new.

Ned Thomas, *The Welsh Extremist*, 1971

834   We hold that to compel Welsh-speaking defendants to submit to trial in English, against their will, before law courts in Wales, is a violation of the rights of man.

G. O. Williams and others, in letter in *The Times*,
26 October 1971

835 I've heard it said that Welsh will live in the home, at the hearth. It's at the hearth it will die if it's not used for all purposes.

Gwyn Williams, in *Artists in Wales*, ed. Meic Stephens, 1971

836 Who speaks for Wales? Nobody. That is both the problem and the encouragement.

Raymond Williams, 'Who speaks for Wales?', in *The Guardian*,
3 June 1971

837 I always order Welsh lamb or mutton in restaurants, in the hope that I'll get to the woolly bastard that keeps tipping my dustbin over.

Anonymous, quoted in Trevor Fishlock,
Wales and the Welsh, 1972

838 The Eisteddfod is the occasion when a lot of Welsh people have a very happy time and there is a great feeling of love and patriotism and a few pretty girls, on a purely temporary basis, you understand, relinquish a little of their virginity.

Trevor Fishlock, *Wales and the Welsh*, 1972

839 I think most Welshmen love Wales more than most Englishmen love England.

840 For all their gloomy analysis, and the Welsh are given to self-examination of the pessimistic kind, history shows that, like their character, their culture has a granite core.

841 There are Welshmen of my acquaintance whose love of their land is uncrushable, who would sing its praises even on the rack.

842 Wales is a meld of differences and there is a tradition of argument.

843 Their hospitality is marvellous and they are the fastest people in the world with the tea-pot, bread-saw and cake-knife.

844 Wales is a split-level country. There is Welsh Wales and English Wales, or if you prefer, not-so-Welsh Wales.

845 Wales, though small, cannot be tidily parcelled. Just as you think you have the picture right, somebody gives the kaleidoscope a nudge and moves the bits.

846   For some of us, you see,
      Wales is another word for peace.

Raymond Garlick, 'Explanatory Note', 1972

847   Although they will probably be horrified to hear it, the thing
which differentiates them from the baboons of the IRA, who blow
the arms and legs off innocent women and children, and break the
knees and tar the bodies of pregnant women, and shoot our lads in
the streets of Londonderry and Belfast, is basically a question of
degree and not kind.

Lord Hailsham, about Cymdeithas yr Iaith Gymraeg, in
address to Welsh Conservatives at Llandrindod Wells, reported in
Western Mail, 24 April 1972

848   The Government already gives practical support in
numerous ways to the Welsh way of life, including the Welsh
language and culture. That support is a continuing process and
wherever new opportunities occur for us to add fruitfully to it, we
shall do so. I think it is a great pity that some of the campaigners
adopt such an aggressive stance, because it is only by tolerance
and friendly co-operation that we can safeguard and strengthen
those characteristics of which the people of Wales are justly
proud.

Edward Heath MP, reported in *Western Mail*, 27 October 1972

849   The art of the possible does not make sense in the present
situation in Wales. The impossible is the only practical way.*

Saunders Lewis, in *Barn*, Christmas 1972

850   The Welsh fall easily into complacency and flatter
themselves interminably, whereas mediocrity is really the chief
mark of what comes out of Wales.

Goronwy Rees, in interview in *Western Mail*, 9 February 1972

851   Wales is still a peasant society in spite of the Industrial
Revolution, and they still have the mentality of peasants.

852   The Welsh admire a victor, but his success always stimulates
their secret resentment, and it is the defeated Cato who really wins
their hearts.

Goronwy Rees, *A Chapter of Accidents*, 1972

853   This fine disregard for legality is something which comes
very easily for the Welsh who, having endured an alien rule for so

long, regard its laws as something which it is a duty to circumvent rather than obey.

854   In choosing the language of my childhood [Welsh], I should have chosen to remain a child for ever, and this is something Welshmen often do.

855   I had thought [of Wales] as the land of a dying language and culture which could no longer satisfy anyone except the very young and the very old.

856   I am being critical of a despair-laden view of Wales generated by a historically motivated nationalism, which because of its very motivation of necessity has to despair of present and future. And I am being critical of it because for my generation it does not correspond with the exciting living reality which we are experiencing now in Wales.

Dafydd Elis Thomas, 'The Images of Wales in R. S. Thomas's
Poetry', in *Poetry Wales*, vol. 7, no. 4, Spring 1972

857   The way I see it around me today, for whoever would be committed to his craft as a writer in Wales now, there can be no peace. There is only war, bitter, prolonged, even violent, through which we must write the truth in the face of all the rotten lies that entangle our lives. Every writer in Wales today is charged with this great responsibility, whatever his language. I believe that sticking to your task can be as valid as going to prison for the language.

Rhydwen Williams, in letter to Meic Stephens, in *Poetry Wales*,
vol. 8, no. 2, Autumn 1972

858   He [the native of north Wales] is usually quite devious, talks as if apple-peel is stuck in his throat and still believes in the Old God.

Ewart Alexander, in *Artists in Wales*, ed. Meic Stephens, 1973

859   I believe a writer, if he looks at Wales, can only write farce or drown in nostalgia for things which aren't there.

860   Despite all the Government assistance that is given to the language in various forms, it cannot be said to be a language policy, any more than the recital of financial incentives to industry can be called a regional policy. Without such a clear lead from Government, which in these days of increasing state intervention must bear a large part of the burden for fostering the language, the

gloomy prospect must be for a running battle with one side
deciding its attitude to each manifestation of the language issue on
an ad hoc basis.

Geraint Talfan Davies, in *Western Mail*, 4 July 1973

861   The language with which all Anglo-Welsh writers are
primarily concerned is naturally English, the problem language of
Wales. For them it is not a provincialising, alienating, London
patois, the sleazy dialect of admass, the insolent cant of the courts;
for them it is one of the mother-tongues of Wales, a classical
language of beauty and precision, used for literary purposes by
some Welshmen for many centuries, a part of the double richness
of Welsh civilization. The problems are how to make it a language
of integration, of reconciliation, of justice.

Raymond Garlick, in *Artists in Wales*, ed. Meic Stephens, 1973

862   I do not consider my not wanting to speak Welsh as a
barrier to understanding. I think that I am in sympathy with the
Welsh language; I like the sound it makes.

Robert Hunter

863   It is puzzling that in Wales, the home of sweeping radical-
ism, we should be so conservative in our music.

Glynne Jones

864   There can be no doubt at all that the Welsh language has
always been the core of our national identity. But I cannot now be
absolutely convinced that it will or need always be so, though I do
believe that even if the language dies it will for centuries to come
have to be accounted as the main factor in shaping whatever
distinctive role we may as a community have yet to play in the
destinies of mankind.

Alun Llywelyn-Williams

865   Have we in the Welsh language ignored the existence of evil
as part of the human condition? This seems to me to be the missing
value that could add the missing dimension to Welsh writing.
Maybe we have emasculated our society by creating around us a
false paradise.

Aled Vaughan

866   My attitude to it [Welsh] is ambiguous: I feel more secure
and relaxed within the sound of it, but when I think about it I'm
sad, for I believe it's going to die, and any nation that lives

through the death of its language lives through an agony of false values, confusion and constricted thinking.

867   The making of Welsh-language [television] programmes is now a legitimate occupation and not a comic pastime. I hope the same can be said of English-language programmes produced in Wales in a decade from now.

868   More and more Welsh signs lead to fewer and fewer Welsh places.

> Ned Thomas, 'Six Characters in Search of Tomorrow', in
> *The Welsh Language Today*, ed. Meic Stephens, 1973

869   Vote Plaid, mun
and be damned for your own sake.

> R. S. Thomas, 'He has the vote', 1973

870   In the past the existence of Ireland, Scotland and Wales has been seen as a threat to the unity of the kingdom centred in London, and in all kinds of subtle ways the prestige of Government and Empire has relegated the Celtic nations to a limbo of the quaint and picturesque cultures that are dead but won't lie down. Now England has to recognize that Britain's future will be far happier and more stable if it accepts the other cultures, not grudgingly but with positive action to sustain their growth.

> G. O. Williams, in *Western Mail*, 1 March 1973

871   Asso asso yogoshi, me Welsh-speaking Japanee.

> Max Boyce, 'Asso asso yogoshi', 1974

872   Bedwellty is not Welsh by language, although Welsh by character and temperament. We have all the essentials of Welsh valley life – clubs and choirs and chapels, and a 22,000 Labour majority.

> Neil Kinnock MP, in speech in the House of Commons,
> 12 March 1974

873   We will meet the genuine demands for new democratic developments with an elected Welsh Assembly.

874   We are the only country in the world where television came before theatre.

> Wilbert Lloyd Roberts, in *Liverpool Daily Post*, 1974

875   What is a Welshman?

R. S. Thomas, title of a book of verse, 1974

876   Taffy has always been a clown and the talent scouts are always on the look-out for new turns.

Harri Webb, in letter to Sam Adams, in *Poetry Wales*,
vol. 10, no. 1, Summer 1974

877   Sing for Wales or shut your trap,
       All the rest's a load of crap.

Harri Webb, 'Advice to a young poet', 1974

878   We beseech you to reconsider your decision to give priority to the English language on bilingual road-signs in Wales. We do so because, like you, we long to see a general disposition in Wales to promote the good of the Welsh language and to put an end to dissension and protest . . . The significance of putting English first will be to proclaim that English is the most highly esteemed language in Wales, and the effect will be to arouse protesters to challenge the law. Feeling certain as we do that this would be as distressing to you as to us, we beg you to change your decision and to give priority to the Welsh language.

G. O. Williams, Archbishop of Wales, and 25 others, in letter to
the Secretary of State for Wales, October 1974

879   When the Anglo-Welsh shake off their awe of the English they may well produce a Neruda or a Paz.

Pennar Davies, in *Poetry Wales*, vol. 11, no. 1, Summer 1975

880   How can we, like the bullet-
       Spattering Mexican, kneel down and give a scooped up
           Handcupful of Welsh soil Zapata's kiss of ecstasy?

Glyn Jones, 'Y Ddraig Goch', 1975

881   Now they're trying to alter all our signposts
           And make us live in streets we cannot say;
       I don't mind the Pakistanis or the Eyties
           But I wish the bleedin' Welsh would stay away.

Graham Jones, 'I'm proud to be a citizen of Kairdiff', 1975

882   Devolutionary reform [for Wales] will not provide a factory, a machine or job, build a school, train a doctor or put a pound on pensions.

Neil Kinnock MP, reported in *South Wales Echo*, 1 November 1975

883 Talk of Welsh to some politicians and county councillors
     And they'll instinctively reach for their consciences.*
                    Gwyn Thomas, 'Soniwch am y Gymraeg', 1975

884 Wales! Whales? D'you mean da fish, or dem singing
bastards?
                    New York taxi-driver, quoted in Trevor Fishlock,
                                        Talking of Wales, 1976

885 Painted green, painted green,
     The signs to heaven were all in Welsh:
     Hell's signs were painted green.
                    Max Boyce, 'The Devil's marking me', 1976

886 My political instincts tell me that the successful implementation of devolution offers us, as a party, the best way of keeping the
United Kingdom united, while at the same time enhancing the
vigour of national diversity within these islands.
                    James Callaghan, in speech to the Labour Party
                                Annual Conference, Brighton, 1976

887 I'm Kairdiff born and I'm Kairdiff bred,
     And when I dies I'll be Kairdiff dead.
                    Frank Hennessy, 'The Kairdiff Song', 1976

888 What is Wales? According to the old nationalism, Wales is
the land from Anglesey to Monmouthshire, the territorial unit on
this side of Offa's Dyke. But I would deny that. This Wales has
ceased to be Wales in the true sense of the word. Only an empty
name remains without the substance of society and neighbour-
hood. House by house, farm by farm, district by district, what you
call Wales has ceased to be a true Wales.*
                    Emyr Llewelyn, *Adfer a'r Fro Gymraeg*, 1976

889 Wales is marching backwards into independence, everybody
desperately pretending that we are going somewhere else.
          Harri Webb, 'Webb's Progress', in *Planet*, no. 30, January 1976

890 The sad fact must be faced that we are even more boring to
the English than they are to us, which is saying a great deal.
                    Harri Webb, 'The Historical Context of Welsh Translation',
                            in *Poetry Wales*, vol. 11, no. 3, Winter 1976

891 Mrs Powell's first cousin had left Patagonia and gone back

home to Wales. 'He *has* done well,' she said. 'He's now the Archdruid.'

Bruce Chatwin, *In Patagonia*, 1977

892   The beach was grey and littered with dead penguins. Halfway along was a concrete monument in memory of the Welsh. It looked like the entrance to a bunker. Let into its sides were bronze reliefs representing Barbarism and Civilization. Barbarism showed a group of Tehuelche Indians, naked, with slabby back muscles in the Soviet style. The Welsh were on the side of Civilization – greybeards, young men with scythes, and big-breasted girls with babies.

893   We have lived with the language neurosis for too long now . . . We have bred a generation of young people to whom Welsh is not an exciting medium of expression but a problem and a worry and a sack of stones on their backs.

T. Glynne Davies, in *Artists in Wales*, ed. Meic Stephens, 1977

894   The survival of a culture, individuality and language are natural matters for Conservative concern. Welsh people, even those who speak only English, are interested in the survival of Welsh, though they do not want it to be the cause of division and privilege.

Nicholas Edwards MP, in speech at the Conservative Party Conference, reported in *The Times*, 13 June 1977

895   The [Welsh] Language Society is still seen by some as a group of hairy Welsh eccentrics, urged on by old men who should know better. But it is more widely regarded as the point of a spear, the personification of a deep actual grievance. It has the support of many writers, academics, teachers and ministers, and there is sympathy for its aims, if not for its methods, from a fairly large section of the Welsh public.

Trevor Fishlock, in *The Times*, 11 November 1977

896   [Wales] must be the only country where one regularly hears nationalists denouncing nationalism.

Tom Nairn, *The Break-up of Britain*, 1977

897   In fact I am a Finn, and Wales is my Finland. I am a Dane, and Wales is my Denmark. I am a Matabele, and Wales is my Zimbabwe.

Dewi Prys-Thomas, in *Artists in Wales*, ed. Meic Stephens, 1977

898   This region [Gwynedd] is a great heartland of Welsh and if it is not defended here of all places it can have no hope of survival. It is not a question of fanaticism. In the first place it is a matter of democracy. A citizen should be able to use the language of his choice.

Ioan Bowen Rees, in *The Times*, 26 July 1977

899   One of the pervading weaknesses of the Anglo-Welsh generally is ghastly good taste.

Harri Webb, in *Artists in Wales*, ed. Meic Stephens, 1977

900   If Wales were to be rolled out as flat as England, it would be the bigger country of the two.

Anonymous, quoted in Christie Davies, *Welsh Jokes*, 1978

901   In answer to a written question, the Secretary of State for Wales told the House of Commons that there had been eight cases of fraud in Carmarthenshire, twelve cases of fraud in Pembrokeshire, and two cases of attempted fraud in Cardiganshire.

902   The Welsh language is so well supplied with good poems it seems unbelievable that it should be in the slightest danger of extinction.

Emyr Humphreys, 'Poetry, Prison and Propaganda', in
Planet, no. 43, June 1978

903   Save the Welsh, Cymry, and you may help to save the world.

904   'You self-righteous, bloody culture-vulture bastard!' said Mick. 'You pathetic self-seeking free-state Plaid Cymru craphouse!' said Ben. 'Come on, then, you reactionary Adfer fascist bum!' said Mick. Connolly shouted, 'Right, boys, stop it! . . . This is a Solidarity Rally!'*

Goronwy Jones, *Dyddiadur Dyn Dŵad*, 1978

905   We cannot afford to flatter nationalism.
Neil Kinnock MP, reported in *South Wales Echo*, 25 February 1978

906   When are knickers panties and when are they briefs?
And how do convictions differ from beliefs?
     Is an inkspot a stain or merely a blot?
     Is a monoglot Welshman Welsh or not?
Peter Elfed Lewis, 'A Question of Definition', 1978

907   In the Wales in which we live, there is no literary answer to
the literary problem. The crisis which is disturbing the nation is
caused by political pressure; it must therefore be resolved
politically.

> R. S. Thomas, 'The Creative Writer's Suicide', in
> *Planet*, no. 41, January 1978

908   Let nobody imagine that because there is so much English in
Wales, it is not a foreign language.

909   Rise up, you Welsh, demand leaders of your own choosing
to govern you, to help you make a future in keeping with your
own best traditions, before it is too late.

910   Our wish is to live at peace with the English, to the point of
servility. They too want to live at peace with us – on their own
terms.

911   We're looking up England's arsehole,
Waiting for the manna to fall.

> Harri Webb, 'Anglo-maniac Anthem', 1978

912   Being Welsh is not merely a predicament, it is as insufferable
as it is inescapable.

> Gwyn A. Williams, *The Merthyr Rising*, 1978

913   We wage, you know, guerrilla war. We avoid confrontation,
we operate by nudge, by conspiracy, by stealth. In Westminster, the
Welsh members wrest, out of the English Establishment, if you like,
they wrest a lot of prizes, as you know, by calling upon the old
cunning which has enabled Wales and its Welshness to survive,
unlike many other territories.

> Leo Abse MP, 'Talking about Devolution', in
> *Planet*, no. 47, February 1979

914   It is our convinced view that the creation of new national
demarcations in Britain through the establishment of separate
Welsh and Scottish Assemblies and new systems of public
expenditure and allocation would divide Britain and the Labour
Movement.

> manifesto of the Labour No Assembly campaign, 1979

915   We have to accept that this concept of a Welsh Assembly is
now dead and buried. However, devolution will not die with this

particular Wales Act. The rejection of the Assembly does not mean that the status quo has been fully endorsed.

editorial in *Western Mail*, 5 March 1979

916   The way forward for Wales is the status quo.

Lord Heycock, quoted by John Osmond in *Planet*, no. 48, May 1979

917   It will be a betrayal of the work of this Government on behalf of Wales for any Socialist to do other than vote Yes.

Cledwyn Hughes MP, in speech in London, 20 February 1979

918   People in South Wales are very charming, but as a crowd they are loud and coarse. We do not want to be governed by Cardiff.

Gwen Mostyn Lewis, in *Western Mail*, 23 March 1979

919   We are asked to tell the Government on St David's Day whether we want a Welsh Assembly or not. The implied question is, Are you a nation or not? May I point out the probable consequences of a No majority? There will follow a general election. There may be a change of government. The first task of a new Westminster Parliament will be to reduce and master inflation. In Wales there are coal mines that work at a loss; there are steelworks that are judged superfluous; there are valleys convenient for submersion. And there will be no Welsh defence.

Saunders Lewis, in letter to *Western Mail*, 26 February 1979

920   When you see an elephant on your doorstep, you know it is there.

John Morris MP, in response to result of Devolution referendum, reported in *Western Mail*, 3 March 1979

921   The metaphor of Wales as a Nonconformist, radical, one-party state, complete with a Welsh-veneered collaborating élite working at long range in London, is rapidly becoming intolerable.

John Osmond, 'Mr Morris and the Elephant', in *Planet*, no. 48, May 1979

922   My father and mother were Welsh-speaking, yet I did not exchange a word in that language with them. The death of Welsh ran through our family of twelve like a geological fault.

Gwyn Thomas, 'The Subsidence Factor', The Gwyn Jones Lecture, 1979

923   In recent centuries we have progressively lost our grip on our own past. Our history has been a history to induce schizophrenia and to enforce loss of memory . . . Half-memories, folklore, myths, fantasy are rampant.

> Gwyn A.Williams, in radio talk, 1979, in *Wales and the Wireless*, ed. Patrick Hannan, 1986

924   Suddenly England, bourgeois England, wasn't my point of reference any more. I was a Welsh European [and] I want the Welsh people – still a radical and cultured people – to defeat, override or by-pass bourgeois England.

> Raymond Williams, *Politics and Letters*, 1979

925   The typical Welsh intellectual is – as we say – only one generation away from shirt sleeves.

926   Why do we in this country spend so much time talking things to destruction?

> Nicholas Edwards MP, in speech to Gwynedd County Council, Llanrwst, 15 April 1980

927   Wales suffers greatly from its stereotypes, often self-inflicted.

> Jan Morris, *My Favourite Stories of Wales*, 1980

928   Old Swansea was never planned. It was doodled over the landscape.

> Wynford Vaughan-Thomas, *Trust to Talk*, 1980

929   Gwynfor 1 Thatcher 0

> graffiti on Thames Embankment opposite House of Commons after the Conservative Government's U-turn on the provision of a Welsh television channel, 1980

930   Wales's greatest tragedy is that she is so far from God and so near to England.

> motion before the Council of Free Churches of North Wales, 1981

931   The Welsh are, and have been, an intensely political nation.

> Kenneth O. Morgan, *Rebirth of a Nation: Wales 1880–1980*, 1981

932   For all that, Wales, like Scotland indeed, also serves as a story of desperate survival against all the odds, of frequent failures

and half-fulfilled aspirations, kept alive without self-destructive bitterness and ultimately with much success.

933   Wales, the first place.

Jan Morris, title of book, 1982

934   Welsh is a life-giving language.

Jan Morris, Wales, the First Place, 1982

935   Nothing is ever settled in Wales. It is a country in flow, always on an ebbing or a rising tide, never actually on the turn.

936   It [the National Eisteddfod] is showy, it is a little senti-mental, some people find it, with its invented antiquities of ritual and costume, rather silly; but it is unmistakably alive.

937   Water is a very Welsh element.

938   The frontiers of a Welsh nation have rarely coincided with the frontiers of a Welsh people.

Gwyn A. Williams, The Welsh in their History, 1982

939   A great deal of Welsh history has been history with the Welsh left out.

940   Welsh identity has constantly renewed itself by anchoring itself in variant forms of Britishness.

941   We are a people with plenty of traditions but no historical memory. We have no historical autonomy. We live in the interstices of other people's history.

942   The form of Welsh personality which historically and genuinely has existed within a British identity seems to carry all the stigmata of the historically transient: it becomes a question of style, of accent, of historically acquired manners, of half-under-stood hymns sung on ritual occasions, a question of trivialities.

943   If capitalism in the British Isles lives, Wales will die. If Wales is to live, capitalism in the British Isles must die.

944   Wales is an artefact which the Welsh produce; the Welsh make and remake Wales day by day and year after year . . . if we want Wales, we will have to make Wales.

945 Britain has begun its long march out of history . . . We Welsh look like being the Last of the British. There is some logic in this. We were, after all, the First.

946 Linguistic nationalism will dissolve us all into warring tribes.
'Land of our Fathers', in *Marxism Today*,
August 1982

947 It is painful and very difficult to create poetry which is relevant in Welsh now. Poets feel very often that it is an act of necrophilia.*
Iwan Llwyd Williams and Wiliam Owen Roberts,
'Myth y Traddodiad Dethol', in
Llais Llyfrau, Autumn 1982

948 The history of Wales, such as it is, is a history of unending resistance and unexpected survival.
Emyr Humphreys, *The Taliesin Tradition*, 1983

949 Let's do our best for the ancient tongue,
Its music's so delightful,
We dearly love to hear it sung,
But speak it? Oh, how frightful!
Harri Webb, 'The Art of the Possible', 1983

950 What Wales needs, and has always lacked most
Is, instead of an eastern boundary, an East Coast.
Harri Webb, 'Our Scientists are Working on it', 1983

951 I think of Wales as my wife and London as my mistress.
Dannie Abse, in *Wales!, Wales?*, broadcast on BBC2,
1 April 1984

952 The Welsh Windbag.
Tariq Ali, of Neil Kinnock, but also applied to
David Lloyd George, 1984

953 Wales is closed.
graffiti on Severn Bridge during miners' strike, 1984/5

954 London flickers in the parlors
of Llansteffan seven nights a week.
Jon Dressel, 'Praise in the Country', 1984

955 He stated his views with great persistence and skill. He was the most powerful opponent we had in Wales.

> Michael Foot MP, of Neil Kinnock's objection to the Labour
> Party's proposals for Devolution, quoted in Robert Harris,
> *The Making of Neil Kinnock*, 1984

956 What opera is to Italy, ballet to Russia, theatre to England, symphonic music to Germany, painting to the Netherlands, poetry is to Wales.

> Raymond Garlick and Roland Mathias, in introduction to
> *Anglo-Welsh Poetry 1480–1980*, 1984

957 Wales hasn't got any history. She hasn't had a history for generations. Bumbling on, surviving from one century to the next . . . Keeping the legends alive, that's all recent Welsh history has been about.*

> Gethin,
> in Aled Islwyn, *Cadw'r Hen Chwedlau'n Fyw*, 1984

958 We are still here! We are still here!
Despite everyone and everything,
We are still here!*

> Dafydd Iwan, 'Yma o Hyd', 1984

959 Wales! Wales?

> Dai Smith, title of book, 1984

960 Wales is a singular noun but a plural experience.
> Dai Smith, *Wales! Wales?*, 1984

961 The recent history of most of the Welsh people is being allowed to drift with them into a lobotomized anonymity.

962 The Wales that is projected to the outside world is not a Wales most of the Welsh know or recognize as anything of their own.

963 Sometimes to live in Wales is to know that the dead still
outnumber the living.
> Duncan Bush, 'The Graveyard in Dinorwic', 1984

964 Wales is infinitely worse off now than it was in 1979, and my view is that this is an argument for devolution, for if we had an elected authority we might have been able to stand up to some of

121

the things that have been happening in Wales, so that to that extent the opponents of devolution were radically wrong in what they did and said.

> Lord Cledwyn in 1984, quoted in Hefin Williams, 'Talking about the Referendum', in *Planet*, no. 72, December/January 1988–9

965   By setting up the Welsh Office, the Labour Government had opened up the floodgates of nationalism.

> George Thomas MP, *Mr Speaker*, 1985

966   The Welsh have always been partial to cheese and forecasts of doom.

> Gwyn Thomas, *High on Hope*, 1985

967   I think the Welsh would have benefited from a spell of totally mindless hedonism.

968   Hearing it [Welsh hymn-singing], I walk again among all those loved and loving people who gave warmth and beauty to the first years of my pilgrimage.

969   Britishness is a mask. Beneath it there is only one nation, England.*

> R. S. Thomas, 'Undod', The J. R. Jones Memorial Lecture, 9 December 1985

970   When was Wales?

> Gwyn A.Williams, title of book, 1985

971   There are roads out towards survival as a people, but they are long and hard and demand sacrifice and are at present unthinkable to most of the Welsh.

> Gwyn A. Williams, *When was Wales?*, 1985

972   One thing I am sure of. Some kind of human society, though God knows what kind, will no doubt go on occupying these two western peninsulas of Britain, but that people, who are my people and no mean people, who have for a millennium and a half lived in them as a Welsh people, are now nothing but a naked people under an acid rain.

973   He's the up-market media Welshman.

> Kingsley Amis, *The Old Devils*, 1986

974   They went outside and stood where a sign used to say Taxi and now said Taxi/Tacsi for the benefit of Welsh people who had never seen a letter x before.

975   Anyway, it was Wales all right . . . There was no obvious giveaway, like road-signs in two languages or closed-down factories, but something was there, an extra greenness in the grass, a softness in the light, something that was very like England and yet not England at all, more a matter of feeling than seeing but not just feeling, something run-down and sad but simpler and freer than England all the same.

976   When Labour councillors in South Wales start blathering about taking modern art to the people, everyone's in deep trouble.

977   Welsh women are culturally invisible.
Deirdre Beddoe, 'Images of Welsh Women', in *Wales: the Imagined Nation*, ed. Tony Curtis, 1986

978   Like the Greeks, the Welsh enjoy their woes and they nourish them in abundance, often preferring remembering to living.
Alun Richards, *Days of Absence*, 1986

979   I know that practically the only growth industry in Wales has been the invention of its own history, forged – in every sense of the word – in the fires of its own powerful fancy.
Ian Skidmore, in radio talk, 1986, in *Wales on the Wireless*, ed. Patrick Hannan, 1986

980   We voted Labour, we got Thatcher.
graffiti in south Wales after General Election, 1987

981   Latterly, with greater knowledge has come better sense. We laugh at the Eisteddfod no longer.
editorial in *The Daily Telegraph*, 10 August 1987

982   Living in Wales is the same as watching the grass grow.*
the pop group Datblygu, 'Gwlad ar fy Nghefn', 1987

983   Because it was so divisive, devolution has been a taboo subject since 1979. Now it's creeping back onto the [Labour Party's] agenda.
Anita Gale, in *Planet*, no. 65, October/November 1987

984   What we in Wales call education
          Marx defined as alienation.
          Chapel too has played its part
          In neutering Fluellen's heart.
               Raymond Garlick, 'Notes for an Autobiography', 1987

985   And certain Welsh electors
          Who (the empire dead) chose to become
          Colonials by referendum.

986   In public and private roles
          A man's life turns on these two poles:
          Survival and identity
          Garrison the heart's warm city.
          On these the life of Wales depends
          Or, with the century, it ends.

987   Leave that Welsh tart alone.
               Mrs Cohen in the film *The Life of Brian*, 1988

988   I think we all have to struggle, to a greater and lesser degree.
It is part of the human condition but is especially true in the Welsh
context. We have to battle against what the Marxists describe as
historical necessity.
               Emyr Humphreys, 'The Dissident Condition', in *Planet*,
                            no. 71, October/November 1988

989   Welsh culture has to be self-confident enough to take on all-
comers. The idea that we can be swamped has to be rejected.
               Dafydd Elis Thomas, quoted by Ned Thomas,
                     'Can Plaid Cymru Survive?', in *Planet*,
                         no. 70, August/September1988

990   I see no other way to unity in Wales except through the
Welsh language. We must start and finish with that, or all our
other efforts will be of no use.*
               R. S. Thomas, *Pe Medrwn yr Iaith*, 1988

991   When I am asked: What is a Welshman? I always answer:
A man who speaks Welsh. I know that many people, particularly
in Glamorgan, believe that to be too restrictive a definition.
Nevertheless, I am of the opinion that to give any other answer is
to set foot on the slippery slope of Britishness.*

992   Wales has largely been defined by forces external to itself.
Gwyn A.Williams, 'Are Welsh Historians putting on the style?',
in *Planet*, no. 68, April/May 1988

993   The Welsh have lived in a permanent state of emergency
since about 383 AD.*
Gwyn A.Williams, in lecture at the National Eisteddfod, 2 August 1988

994   We as a people have been around for two thousand years.
Isn't it about time we got the key to our own front door?
Gwyn A.Williams, in speech to the Campaign for a Welsh
Assembly, Merthyr Tydfil, 26 November 1988

995   We have a border in Wales. No one proposes to make it a
Berlin Wall, but it exists. Everything west of that line is Wales,
everyone west of that line who commits herself or himself to Wales
is a member of the Welsh people. I don't care what language they
speak. I don't care what colour their faces are, I don't care where
they come from. If they live in Wales and count themselves Welsh,
they are Welsh people.

996   The politicians have failed to defend the rights of the Welsh
people. We therefore announce that all white settlers are targets
for Meibion Glyndŵr. The colonists must understand that this is
the land of the Welsh and not their last colony. We shall bury
English imperialism.*
statement by Meibion Glyndŵr, signed 'Rhys Gethin' (one of
Owain Glyndŵr's captains), 1 March 1989

997   In times past the Principality has always been a culinary
graveyard where cooking standards in hotels, restaurants, pubs and
farmhouses were as grim as gravestones in Welsh cemeteries.
Richard Binn, *A Taste of Wales*, 1989

998   My wife died of cirrhosis of the liver. She was Welsh, and
drink never did the Welsh any good – think of Dylan Thomas and
Richard Burton.
Anthony Burgess, in *Sunday Times*, 19 February 1989

999   One day devolved power will return to Scotland, Wales and
Ulster. The United Kingdom will be re-pluralised. But goodness
knows how much crockery will be smashed in the mean time.
Simon Jenkins, 'Nationalists chafe under an alien yoke',
in *Sunday Times*, 2 April 1989

1000   Wales, unlike Ireland, has never quite caught the English Left's ear. It is as if the propinquity and sustained ambiguity of Wales is too much, too close, to grasp for those who can only hear distant trumpets.

Dai Smith, 'Relating to Wales', in *Raymond Williams: Critical Perspectives*, ed. Terry Eagleton, 1989

1001   On 1 March 1979 Scotland and Wales went to the polls on Devolution. The cause of home rule had been totally damaged by a close identification with a deeply unpopular Labour Government. A poll on Devolution became a referendum on Labour.

David Steel MP, 'A Single Vote Landslide', in the *Independent*, 28 March 1989

1002   After 1992 we will be citizens of Europe, not citizens of the UK. We will have burgundy-coloured passports and pink European driving-licences. We will have to see ourselves more and more as Welsh Europeans.

Dafydd Elis Thomas MP, reported in *Western Mail,* 2 March 1989

1003   I have always refused to be labelled as a Welsh Nationalist. It is not a coherent philosophy.

Dafydd Elis Thomas MP, in *Tribune*, 14 April 1989

1004   Only a novelist could do justice to the extraordinary country we live in . . . below the surface stereotypes of rugby and shepherds and choirs lies a most intricate pattern of power and patronage, most of them depending in the end on London for their influence.

Ned Thomas, 'Man who set the ball rolling at S4C', in *Wales on Sunday*, 4 June 1989

1005   Clearly the struggle to defend Welsh democracy at home and to advance it in Europe are one struggle. The enemy is the same: the separatist and authoritarian British state. It is not enough to capture that Bastille: we have to dismantle it brick by brick.

Gwyn A.Williams, in editorial in *Radical Wales*, no. 21, Spring 1989

1006   We bring up our children to speak Welsh not for the sake of the language, but for the sake of our children.

Ioan Bowen Rees, 'Wales Today: Nation or Market?', in *Planet*, no. 79, February/March 1990

1007 We can take little comfort from the fact that, in principle, almost everyone is in favour of Welshness and of the language: all the enemies of Welsh have to do is nothing.

1008 There is always the danger of a small nation under the thumb of a large state becoming a nation of boot-lickers. The rise of the quango in Wales today is a continuous threat to self-respect.

1009 We come to see ourselves as Welsh, and to make our commitment to Wales, for different reasons and in different ways, and there seems to be little point in falling out over it. Perhaps, instead, we should try now to accept the differences and go on to explore what we have in common and what we might yet make of it.

> Meic Stephens, 'In John Jones's Country', in *Planet*,
> no. 82, August/September 1990

1010 Soon what is right for Sofia and for Riga may begin to make sense in Cardiff. And the top-heavy bureaucracy of the Welsh Office will collapse under its own weight into a form of new democracy even in Wales. Then and only then will we as a people become part of the modern world and the twenty-first century.

> Dafydd Elis Thomas MP, 'Democracy should rule here as well',
> in *Western Mail,* 3 January 1990

1011 Even at the end of the twentieth century, the language, absent or present, remains the key to the Welsh condition.

> Emyr Humphreys, 'A Lost Leader?', in *Planet*,
> no. 83, October/November 1990

1012 We are ruled from Westminster and have been for centuries. The Act of Union of 1536 is a misnomer. By that Act, Wales was annexed to and incorporated in the English State. The Welsh language has been looked upon as an administrative nuisance ever since.

> R. S. Thomas, 'Reflections on a Speech at Machynlleth', in
> *Planet*, no. 84, December 1990/January 1991

1013 Wales does not belong to London any more. The truth is, it never did.

> Tudor David, 'The Rise and Fall of the London Welsh', in
> *Planet*, no. 85, February/March 1991

1014 It is quite safe for the Welsh to think of themselves as poets, preachers, singers and sportsmen. But what if the truth came out: that the Welsh are really a nation of scientists, engineers and entrepreneurs? Why, the next thing would be that the Welsh would lose their inferiority complex! Good heavens, we might even start thinking that Wales was not a backward province but a nation with a proud tradition and quite capable of governing itself.

Phil Williams, 'Land of Poets and Scientists', in *Planet*,
no. 85, February/March 1991

1015   Wales has usually been defined [in England] by a series of quaint images based on the film version of *How Green Was My Valley* and pictures of elderly men dressed as druids.

Glyn Davies, 'The Face in the Mirror', in *Planet*,
no. 90, December 1991/January 1992

1016   Welsh rugby, once a source of national pride, has now become part of that rapid erosion of identity which has thrown a big question-mark over what it means to be Welsh today.

1017   The time is long overdue for the creation of a directly elected Welsh Assembly with effective decision-making powers over the whole range of Welsh policy under the control of the Welsh Office.

Campaign for a Welsh Assembly, reported in *Western Mail*,
2 April 1992

1018   This English need to play down and despise all things Welsh appears to come from some deep complex that is beyond the reach of reason. Do they feel some ancient resentment that they were not the first people on this island or do they simply resent a group that does not accept automatically everything they stand for?

Richard Jones, 'The Kebabbing of Neil Kinnock', in
The New Welsh Review, no. 17, Summer 1992

1019   There is no doubt that the general status of Welsh has improved immensely during the ten years of S4C's existence.

Ned Thomas, 'Ten Years On', in *Planet*,
no. 96, December 1992/January 1993

1020   Tourism is now the most important Welsh industry, and tourism is doing its level best to destroy what many people consider the two essential characteristics of Wales – its environment and its culture.

Robert Minhinnick, *A Postcard Home*, 1993

1021   This appointment [of John Redwood as Secretary of State for Wales] will be resented even by Tories in Wales. It is abundantly clear that John Major has written off the Tory Party in Wales, accepting that they have no mandate, by replacing an out-of-touch Governor General [David Hunt] with a city slicker.

Ron Davies MP, reported in *Western Mail*,
28 May 1993

1022   Welsh is an official language in this country. That does not have to be stated in law. It is not stated in law in respect of English. English is also an official language.

Sir Wyn Roberts MP, in speech in House of Commons,
15 July 1993

1023   Let's have more debates about the future political system of Wales and Europe through the medium of Welsh, but the fate of the language itself must be above that debate. It should be the vehicle, not the cause of it.

Lord Dafydd Elis-Thomas, quoted in *Western Mail*,
26 October 1993

1024   An Act to establish a Board having the function of promoting and facilitating the use of the Welsh language, to provide for the preparation by public bodies of schemes giving effect to the principle that in the conduct of public business and the administration of justice in Wales the English and Welsh languages should be treated on a basis of equality, to make further provision relating to the Welsh language, to repeal certain spent enactments relating to Wales, and for connected purposes.

full title of the Welsh Language Act, 1993

1025   Democracy is the rock on which the people of Wales set their demand for an elected Parliament.

Tom Ellis, 'Putting the People First', in *A Parliament for Wales*,
ed. John Osmond, 1994

1026   Wales today is a great deal less democratic than in 1945. With the rise of the quangos and the sharp decline in the democratic powers of local government, a Parliament for Wales needs to be more than a glorified County Council.

Hywel Francis, 'Strangers in our Own Land?'

1027   During the 1990s and especially since the 1992 general election, I have noticed a sea-change in favour of a Welsh

Parliament within my constituency in Neath and, indeed, across Wales. There are three main reasons. The democratic case becomes ever stronger as the Tories ride roughshod over our democratic rights in Wales. There is the growing importance of the European dimension in our affairs. And there is a growing realization that it is economically more successful to devolve power.

Peter Hain MP, 'Empowering the People'

1028   Wales in the 1990s is a very different place from the Wales of the 1970s.

John Osmond, 'Remaking Wales'

1029   The young Welsh citizens of the future will need to be locally rooted with a sense of security in their ideas of Wales. But they will also have to be at ease as citizens of the European Union. These are not alternatives. We need a Parliament for Wales to ensure that the vision of a national identity merges with an international consciousness for our young people becomes a reality.

David Reynolds, 'Building our National Identity'

1030   A Welsh Parliament will ensure that policies favoured by a majority of the people of Wales are followed. It will build a better future for our people by placing emphasis on economic regeneration and the provision of work. It will give us the freedom and responsibility to renew our culture and express our unity, national identity, and cultural diversity.

declaration of the Llandrindod Democracy Conference,
March 1994

1031   If an Englishman enters a shop in Welsh-speaking parts of Wales, the locals are likely to switch promptly to speaking Welsh. Thus the Englishman cannot be sure whether they are talking about him.

John Redwood MP, *The Global Marketplace:Capitalism and its Future*, 1994

1032   Like the Scots, we are a nation. We have our own country. We have our own language, our own history, traditions, ethics, values and pride . . . We now demand the right to decide through our own democratic institutions the procedures and the structures and the priorities of our own civic life.

Ron Davies MP, in speech to Labour Party Conference, 1994

1033   Cardiff: half-and-half a capital.

Rhodri Morgan MP, title of pamphlet, 1994

1034   Labour is committed to legislating for a democratic Welsh Assembly in the first year of winning office. . . Once the Assembly is established it must reflect the diversity and plurality of Welsh social, political and cultural life.

Ron Davies MP, in speech at Treorchy, January 1995

1035   English is a Welsh language in which nothing flourishes.

Karl Francis, 'English is a Welsh Language Too', in
Towards the Millennium, 1995

1036   The [Welsh Language Board] was appointed by a Secretary of State for Wales who represented a constituency in Conservative England and who refused to sign official documents written in Welsh.

Dylan Iorwerth, 'Full Hearts and Empty Vessels',
in *A Week in Europe*, 1995

1037   Could Welsh become the language of officialdom but not of real life?

1038   Welsh politics revolve around a contradiction that while the Labour Party consistently wins a majority of seats and nearly half the vote, more often than not the Conservatives rule Wales on the basis of the support they receive in southern England.

John Osmond, *Welsh Europeans*, 1995

1039   Not since Caligula made his horse senator has there been such a ridiculous appointment.

John Morris MP, of the appointment of William Hague as
Secretary of State for Wales, reported in
Western Mail, 6 July 1995

1040   The institution of an English Prince of Wales, son to the English monarch, is (to be frank at last) a dead loss. It is meaningless, silly and insulting. The sooner Prince Charles himself accepts the fact – and he must surely be aware of it already – the better for everyone.

Jan Morris, *The Princeship of Wales*, 1995

1041   John Redwood's callow colonialism as Welsh Secretary probably did a good turn for the cause of a Welsh Parliament. At least it drew attention to the undemocratic nature of Welsh government.

Tom Ellis, 'The British Case for a Welsh Parliament', in *Planet*, no. 114, December 1995/January 1996

1042   The road to a Welsh hell will be paved with the good intentions of Labour's devolutionists.

Tim Williams, in *Western Mail*, June 1996

1043   Ask most people in Wales what sticks in their minds about John Redwood's stint at the Welsh Office [as Secretary of State for Wales] and they mention two things: Redwood's mouthing of the national anthem (and looking like a turkey pretending to sing a Christmas carol), and his denouncing the unmarried mothers of St Mellons.

Nerys Thomas Patterson, 'Welsh Bastards and Washington', in *Planet*, no. 118, August/September 1996

1044   Rugby. Tom Jones. Male Voice Chairs. Shirley Bassey. Llanfairpwllgwyngyllgogerythgwynrobollantisilioagogogoch [*sic*]. Snowdonia. Prince of Wales. Anthony Hopkins. Daffodils. Sheep. Sheep Shaggers. Coal. Slate Quarries. The Blaeanau [*sic*] Ffestiniog Dinkey Dooey Miniature Railway . . . Now if that's your idea of thousands of years of Welsh culture, you can't blame us for trying to liven the place up a little bit, can you?

from the film *Twin Town*, 1997

1045   Destroying the British political system through devolution will bring no gains to the Welsh people.

Tim Williams, *The Patriot Game*, 1997

1046   Today, unless we pull back from the edge, we will be ruled from Cardiff, Edinburgh and yes, Brussels. If your heart rejoices at the prospect, vote for devolution. If your heart missed a beat when you read that, vote No. Positively No. Be radical: support the status quo.

1047   Good-morning – and it is a very good morning in Wales.

Ron Davies MP, in speech after Devolution referendum result, 19 September 1997

1048   One Ron Davies, there's only one Ron Davies.

crowd singing in Park Hotel, Cardiff, 19 September 1997

1049   Wales says Yes!

headline in *Western Mail*, 19 September 1997

1050   Among the most exciting possibilities offered by the Assembly will be the prospect of forging a new national unity out of the rich mixture of race, colour, class and culture that is Wales.

Mario Basini, in *Western Mail*, 20 September 1997

1051   We gave Ron Davies a run for his money.

Carys Pugh, of the No campaign, reported in *Western Mail*, 20 September 1997

1052   Believe me, a department that answers to sixty politicians who in turn answer to people from all over Wales is going to respond very differently from that which answers to one Cabinet Minister, whoever he or she is . . . We are going to have to get used to explaining ourselves in public.

Rachel Lomax, in speech to Institute of Welsh Affairs, 7 November 1997

1053   Every day when I wake up I thank the Lord I'm Welsh.

Mark Roberts/Catatonia, 'International Velvet', 1998

1054   Any thought of a battle for the Welsh language is certainly over. The battle between Welsh-speakers and the authorities for greater provision of services in Welsh has largely been won.

Rhodri Williams, reported in *Western Mail*, February 1998

1055   When I started out as a young councillor in the Rhymney Valley, the Welsh language was a hot potato which aroused angst and ire all over Wales. It was something you were either 'for' or 'against': there wasn't much room for neutrality. But now that mode of thinking has been largely abandoned. Whether you happen to speak Welsh or not, there is increasingly the view that the language is part of what makes our identity as a nation distinctive and unique. The language is no longer a political football in the way it once was.

Ron Davies MP, reported in *Western Mail*, 2 July 1998

1056   Wales has a National Assembly because it is a Nation. The powers of the National Assembly have been restricted in case Wales acts as a Nation.

Phil Williams, *The Welsh Budget*, 1998

1057   Young people have always been ignored in Welsh-speaking Wales. But suddenly, it has become more important to create a Welsh youth culture than it ever was. What has happened? A National Assembly is about to be established – a turning-point in our history. From now on, Welshness will be defined by the new political entity. People will not be prepared to use Welsh just because it is a relic from the past. Unless we create a contemporary and relevant culture in the national language, then – just as in Ireland – it will disappear.*

Simon Brooks, *Diwylliant Poblogaidd*, 1998

1058   The Welsh Language Society calls upon the National Assembly of Wales to operate a language policy which recognises Welsh as the language proper to Wales, both Welsh and English as official working languages of the Assembly, and to use the other languages of Wales, the languages of the European Union, and any other languages as appropriate.

Welsh Language Society, *A Working Bilingualism*, 1998

1059   Devolution is a process, not an event and neither is it a journey with a fixed end-point.

Ron Davies MP, *Devolution: A Process not an Event*, 1999

1060   I didn't like what I saw in Welsh politics at Westminster. I regarded it as a snake-pit.

1061   I wanted to rebrand Wales and notions of Welshness to reflect the real living modern Wales, to establish the idea of Wales as a vibrant, diverse, tolerant and outward-looking country with an internationalist spirit.

1062   Our devolved settlement represents a new partnership between Wales and the United Kingdom. Wales is just as much part of the United Kingdom as it ever was. In the future, however, we will have to take responsibility for our own actions. We can no longer look to London to cast blame.

1063   The new Welsh politics is about creating a new democracy and a new civil society to make the democracy work. When it first meets, the National Assembly will not be representative of that civil society. But it will be the essential instrument to ensure that in the coming decades a Welsh democracy and a Welsh civil society will come into being.

John Osmond, in *The National Assembly Agenda*, 1999

1064   On 6 May 1999, we shall be electing the first members of our National Assembly. Within days, Wales will have its own government and a distinct political and constitutional identity, for the first time in six hundred years. That, in itself, despite all the restrictions on the Assembly's powers, is a cause for joy and pride to a nation which has for so long walked in the shadows, deprived of status and dignity.*

Dewi Watkin Powell, *Cynulliad i Genedl*, 1999

1065   Confidence is a wonderful state of mind. The Welsh team now has it in abundance and, more importantly, it has rubbed off on the rest of the nation. It's a day to be proud.

editorial in *Western Mail*, after Wales beat England at rugby 32:31, 12 April 1999

1066   As long as we beat the English we don't care.

Kelly Jones of the Stereophonics, BBC Wales, April 1999

1067   Let no one think that now the devolution genie is out of his bottle he can be forced back in or that he will not want to stretch his muscles.

Ron Davies MP, in preface to *Scotland and Wales: Nations Again?*, ed. Bridget Tayor and Katarina Thomson, 1999

1068   Politics and government in Wales have changed forever.

1069   Only Labour had the strength and organisation to deliver change in Wales, but with that power should have come the recognition that we do not have a monopoly of wisdom.

1070   Plaid Cymru has never advocated independence – never, ever, on any occasion.

Dafydd Wigley MP, 13 April 1999

1071   Labour paid the price yesterday for its arrogance, sloth, incompetence and frequent corruption across huge swathes of Wales.

editorial in *Western Mail*, on the results of the first election to the National Assembly, 8 May 1999

Index
Authors and anonymous sources

Gee, Thomas 297
Genedl Gymreig, Y 341
Gerald of Wales, *see* Giraldus
    Cambrensis
Gildas 6, 7
Giraldus Cambrensis 24, 29–42
Gladstone, William Ewart 319,
    327, 334, 335, 353
Glaslyn, *see* Jones, Richard
Graves, Robert 519, 520
Griffith, Llewelyn Wyn 590–3, 609,
    644, 645
Griffiths, James 608, 684
Griffiths, John 296
Gruffudd, Robat 795
Gruffydd, Peter 784
Gruffydd, W. J. 507, 508, 510–12,
    515, 524, 526, 539, 547, 548, 563,
    568–70, 594, 623, 638
Guest, Lady Charlotte 206, 208–10
Guto'r Glyn 68, 69
Gwilym Hiraethog, *see* Rees,
    William
Gwladgarwr, Y 289

Hailsham, Lord 847
Hain, Peter 1027
Hardie, Keir 362, 399, 400, 422,
    440, 441
Harris, John 474
Hawthorne, Nathaniel 263
Heath, Edward 848
Heddiw 566, 586, 598
Hemans, Felicia Dorothea 201
Henderson, Arthur 478
Hennessy, Frank 887
Henry II 25
Heycock, Lord 916
Historia Anglicana 54
Historia Brittonum 18
Hooson, Emlyn 718
Hopkins, Gerard Manley 320
Horner, Arthur 632
Housman, A. E. 374
Hughes, Cledwyn 654, 740, 917,
    964
Hughes, Ernest 493
Hughes, H. M. 401

Hughes, John Ceiriog 270, 271,
    305, 336
Hughes, Richard 646
Humphreys, Emyr 806, 807, 902,
    903, 948, 988, 1011
Humphries, Rolfe 699, 700
Hunter, Robert 862

Ieuan Brydydd Hir, *see* Evans,
    Evan
Ieuan Gwynedd, *see* Jones, Evan
Iolo Morganwg, *see* Williams,
    Edward
Iorwerth, Dylan 1036, 1037
Islwyn, Aled 957
Iwan, Dafydd 958

James, David Emrys (Dewi Emrys)
    513
James, Evan 265
Jenkins, John 822, 823
Jenkins, R.T. 776
Jenkins, Simon 999
Jevons, Stanley 459
John de Weston 60
John, Augustus 402
Johnson, Arthur Tyssilio 423–35
Johnson, Samuel 139
Jones, Basil 332
Jones, Bobi 672, 796, 797
Jones, David 709
Jones, D. Gwenallt 564
Jones, Edward 164
Jones, E. Pan 343
Jones, Ernest 719
Jones, Evan (Ieuan Gwynedd) 251
Jones, Glyn 610, 785, 786, 880
Jones, Glynne 863
Jones, Goronwy 904
Jones, Graham 881
Jones, Griffith 129
Jones, Griffith Hartwell 624
Jones, Gwyn 571, 572, 625, 703–7
Jones, Henry 337
Jones, Idrisyn 375
Jones, John 192
Jones, John M. 475, 476
Jones, J. R. 808–10

Saunders, Erasmus 122
Savage, Richard 126
Scott, Sir Walter 177, 188
Shakespeare, William 92–9
Shaw, George Bernard 455, 456
Shelley, Percy Bysshe 179, 180
Sidney, Sir Henry 81
Sidney, Sir Philip 91
Simon, Glyn 789, 798
Skidmore, Ian 979
Smith, Dai 959–62, 1000
Smith, F. E. 484
Snowden, Mrs Philip 386
Socialists of Llanelly Hill 380
Southey, Robert 212
Speaker's Conference on
    Devolution (1920) 485
Spring, H. L. 303, 304
Statute of Rhuddlan 52
Steel, David 1001
Stereophonics, *see* Jones, Kelly
Stephens, Meic 743–6, 779–82, 1009
Stephens, Thomas 412

Tacitus 2, 3
Taliesin 10
Thomas, D. Lleufer 462
Thomas, Dafydd Elis *see* Elis-
    Thomas, Dafydd
Thomas, David 356
Thomas, Dylan 538, 612, 686, 694,
    695
Thomas, Edward 463, 469
Thomas, George 829, 965
Thomas, Gwyn (novelist) 714, 739,
    747, 758, 764, 768–71, 817, 830,
    831, 922, 966–8
Thomas, Gwyn (poet) 883
Thomas, Ned 814–16, 832, 833,
    868, 1004, 1019
Thomas, R. S. 628–30, 636, 664,
    665, 676, 677, 731, 732, 748, 790,
    791, 799, 869, 875, 907–10, 969,
    990, 991, 1012
Thomas, T. H. 413
Thomas, T. J. (Sarnicol) 544
Times, The 286, 287, 288, 313, 453,
    514

Tolkien, J. R. R. 696
Torbuck, John 131
Trevelyan, Marie 359
Twin Town 1044

Urdd Gobaith Cymru 490

Vanbrugh, John 118
Vaughan, Aled 865–7
Vaughan, Hilda 505
Vaughan, Rowland 108
Vaughan-Thomas, Wynford 928
Victoria, Queen 253, 346
Vincent, Henry 216
Vita Edwardi Secundi 58
Vivian, Hussey 280

Wade-Evans, A. W. 583, 584
Walters, John 135
Warner, Richard 160
Watkins, Vernon 631, 733
Watson, Sir William 421
Waugh, Evelyn 517, 518
Webb, Harri 720, 749, 800–2. 876,
    877, 889, 890, 899, 911, 949, 950
Welsh Courts Act (1942) 597
Welsh Language Act (1967) 775
Welsh Language Act (1993) 1024
Welsh Language Society, *see*
    Cymdeithas yr Iaith Gymraeg
Welsh League of Youth, *see* Urdd
    Gobaith Cymru
Welsh Outlook 470, 471, 480, 481,
    488, 506, 525
Welsh Republican, The 642, 643, 648
Welsh Review, The 620
Wesley, John 128, 142
Western Mail 331, 482, 683, 774,
    915, 1049, 1065, 1071
Wheeler, Mortimer 697, 698
White, Gilbert 147
White, Walter 269
Whitman, Walt 347
Widgery, Justice 772
Wigley, Dafydd 1070
Williams, David 153
Williams, D. J. 616, 659, 678, 750,
    792

Index

People and places